Harmonica Tunes

Beautiful Airs and Ballads of the British Isles

Phil Duncan

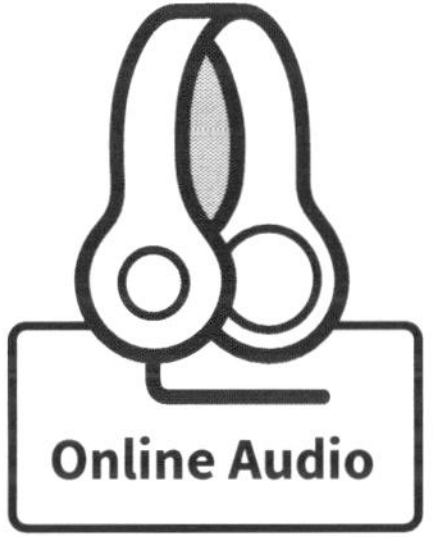

To Access the online audio go to:
WWW.MELBAY.COM/30951MEB

The HOHNER Special 20 harmonica image on the cover is courtesy of HOHNER Musikinstrumente GmbH.

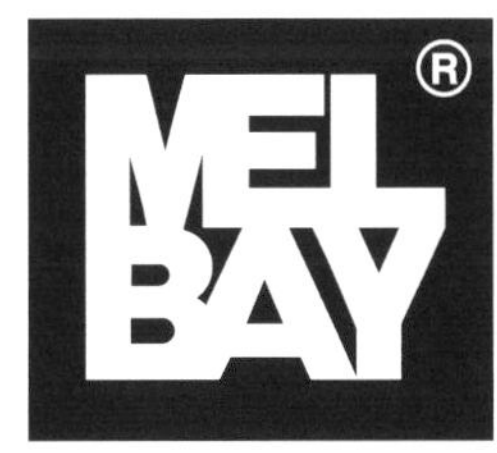

WWW.MELBAY.COM

Preface

The music of the British Isles is so intrenched in American culture that its influence cannot be ignored. Many of these melodies have provided the seeds that established the musical environment that surrounds us to this day. While they have a familiar air about them, these wonderful tunes are charming and relatively easy to play. All you need is a standard diatonic harmonica in the key of C, and you are good to go.

The 15 solo harmonica tunes that comprise this book approximate the approach my grandfather gave me when I was a boy, presenting engaging tunes to encourage rapid progress. This music has certainly enriched my life, and now I want to share it with you.

All the music in this book is presented in standard notation and blow/draw harmonica tablature with suggested chords. You can play these tunes as unaccompanied solos, or with a friend on guitar or any instrument with chord capability. If you also play the guitar, you can use a rack to hold the harmonica while you accompany yourself.

For ease of learning I have included online recordings.

Index

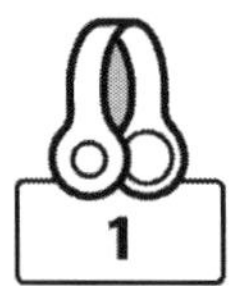

Annie Laurie (Scottish)

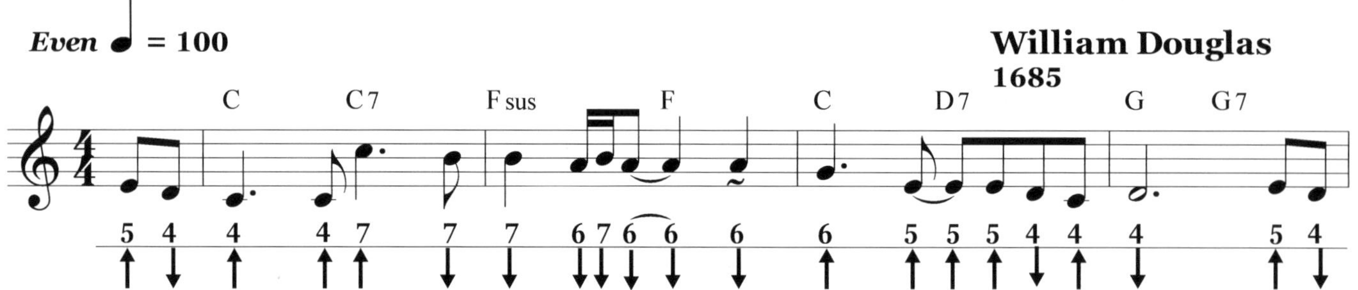

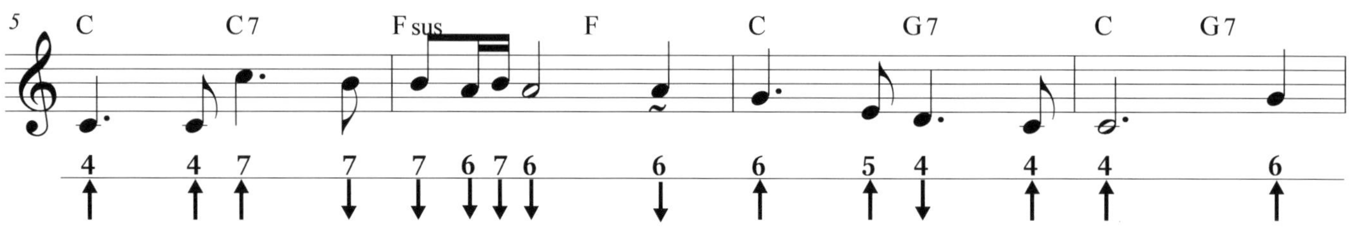

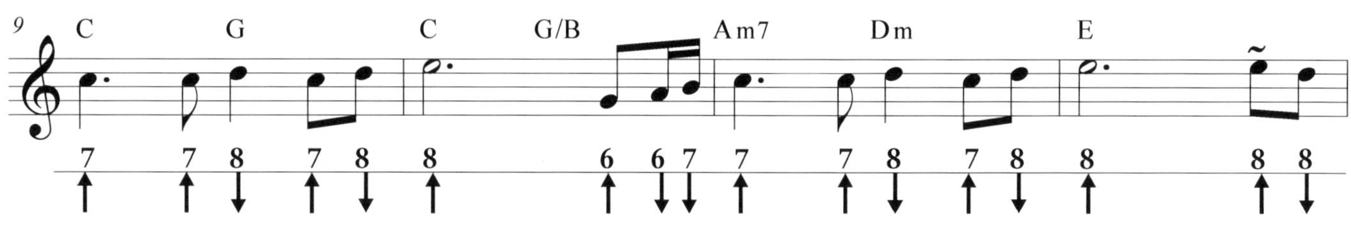

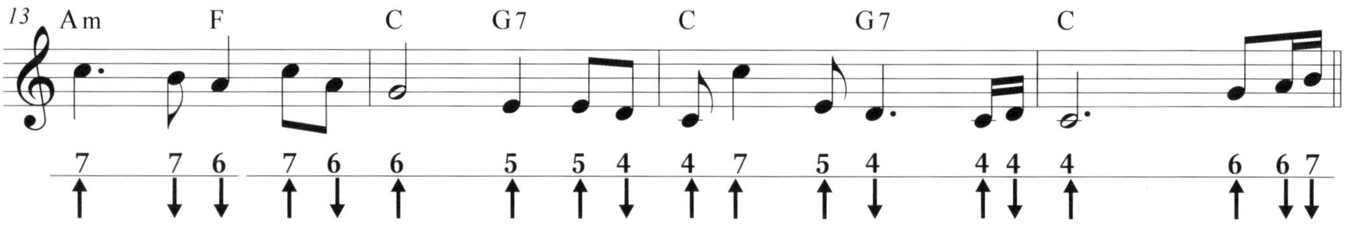

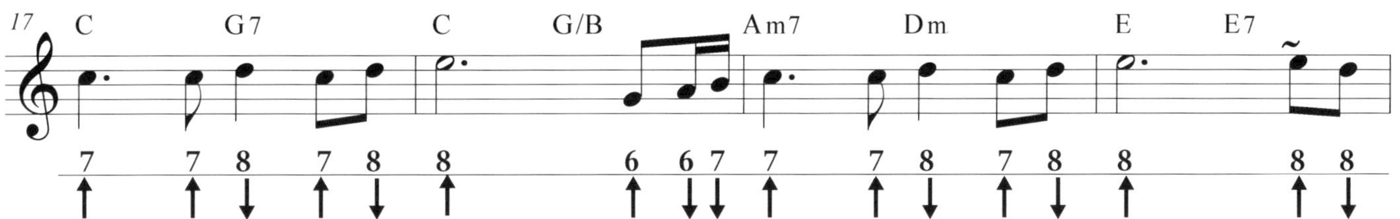
17
C G7 C G/B Am7 Dm E E7
7 7 8 7 8 8 6 6 7 7 7 8 7 8 8 8 8

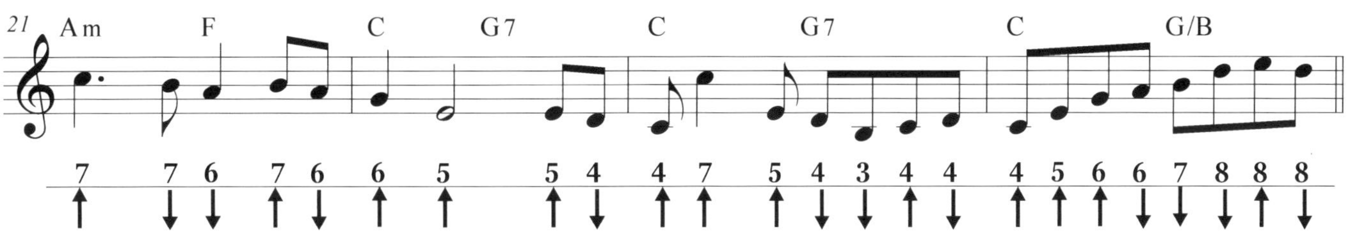
21
Am F C G7 C G7 C G/B
7 7 6 7 6 6 5 5 4 4 7 5 4 3 4 4 4 5 6 6 7 8 8 8

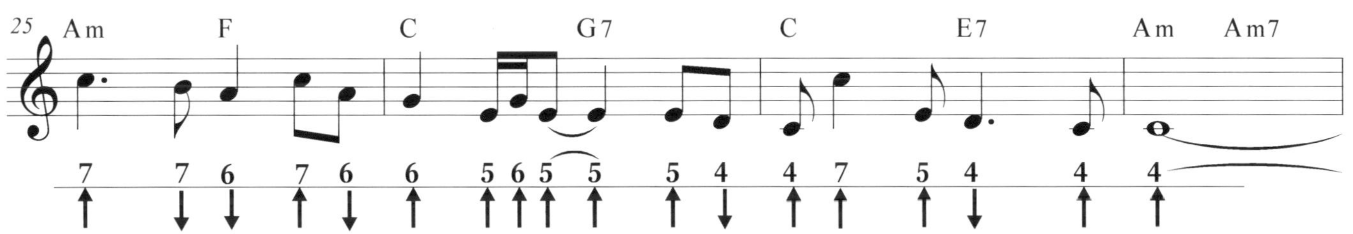
25
Am F C G7 C E7 Am Am7
7 7 6 7 6 6 5 6 5 5 5 4 4 7 5 4 4 4

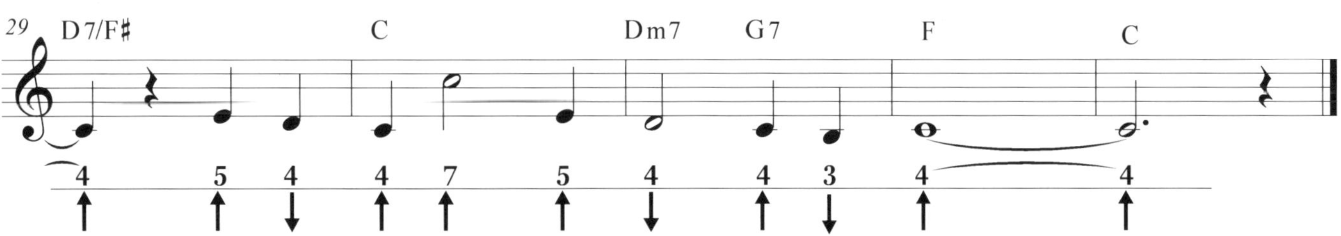
29
D7/F♯ C Dm7 G7 F C
4 5 4 4 7 5 4 4 3 4 4

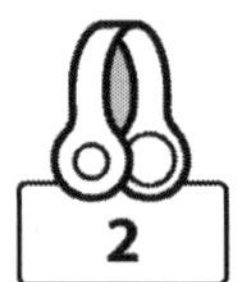

The Blue Bells of Scotland

(A symbol of beauty, a sweet flower)

Dora Jordon,
1762-1816
Arr. P. Duncan

Even ♩ **= 110**

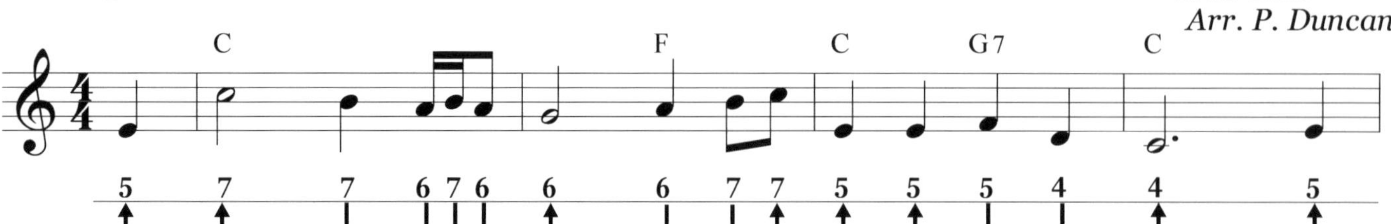

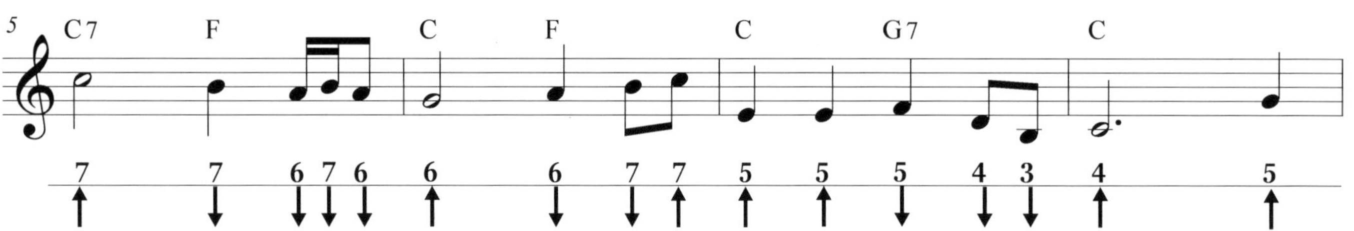

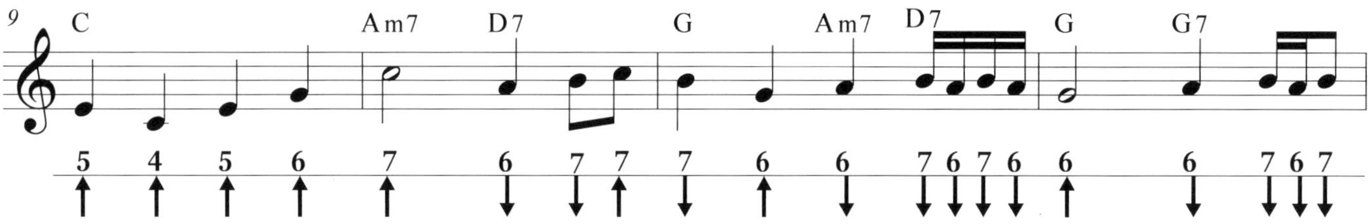

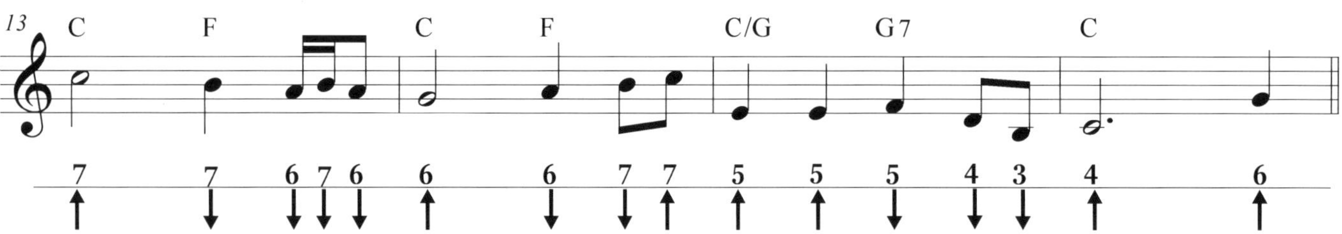

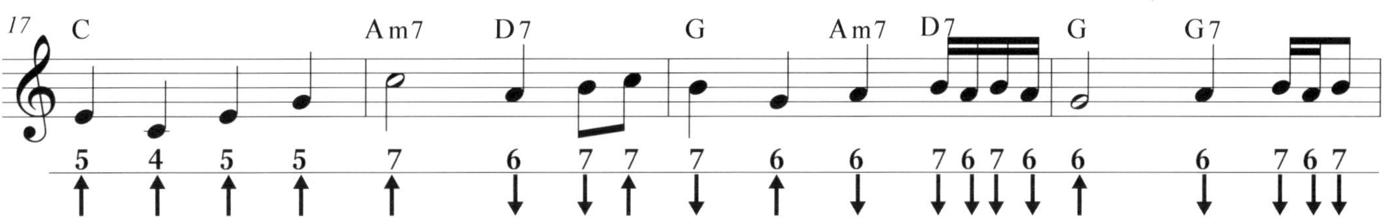
17
C Am7 D7 G Am7 D7 G G7
5 4 5 5 7 6 7 7 7 6 6 7 6 7 6 6 6 7 6 7

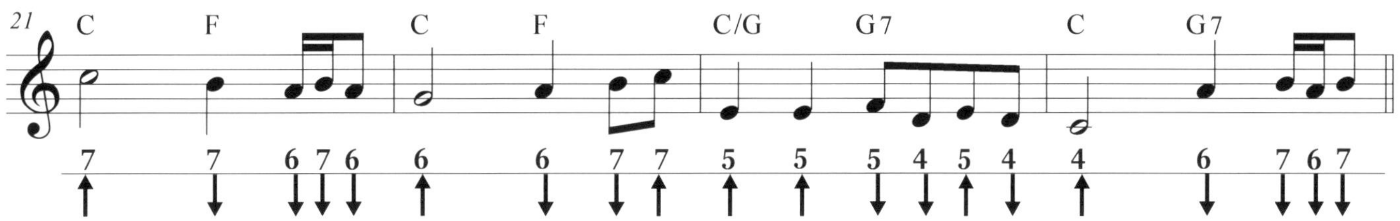
21
C F C F C/G G7 C G7
7 7 6 7 6 6 6 7 7 5 5 5 4 5 4 4 6 7 6 7

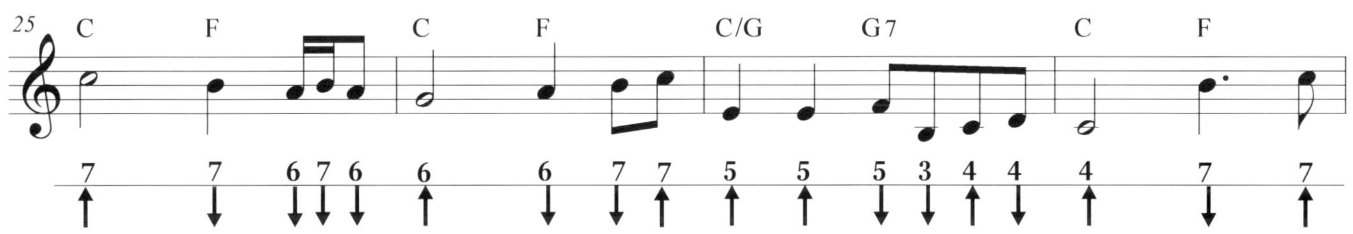
25
C F C F C/G G7 C F
7 7 6 7 6 6 6 7 7 5 5 5 3 4 4 4 7 7

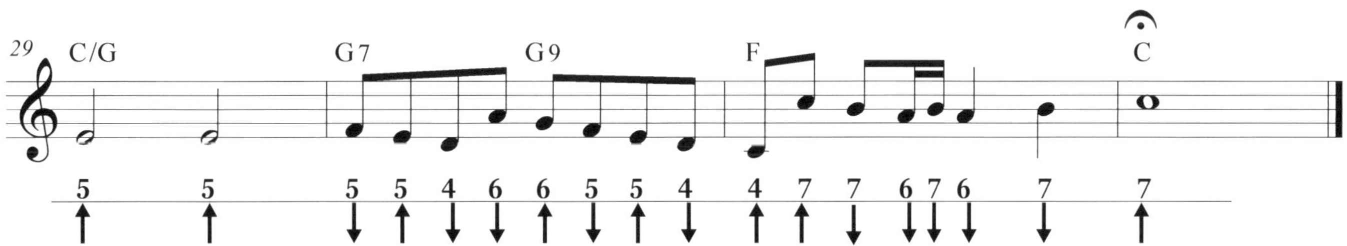
29
C/G G7 G9 F C
5 5 5 5 4 6 6 5 5 4 4 7 7 6 7 6 7 7

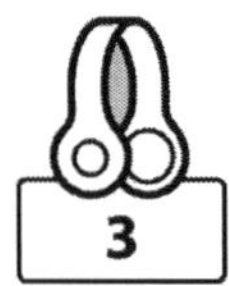

The Bailiff's Daughter of Islington

Even **♩ = 105** **English Ballad**

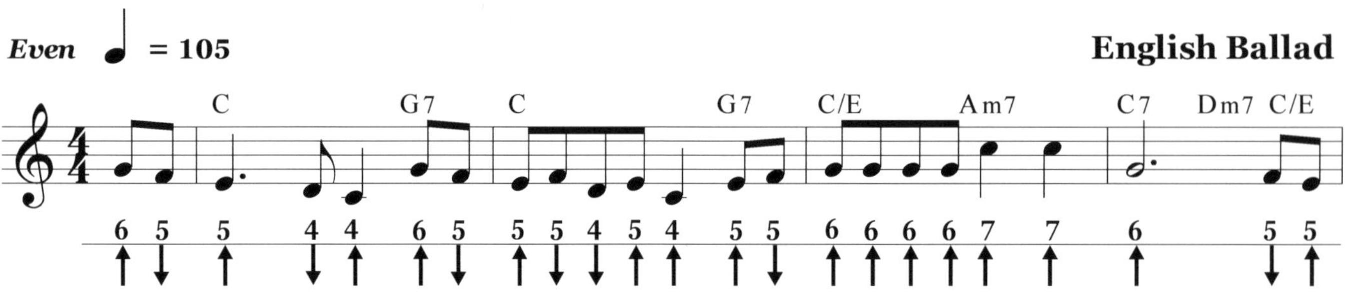

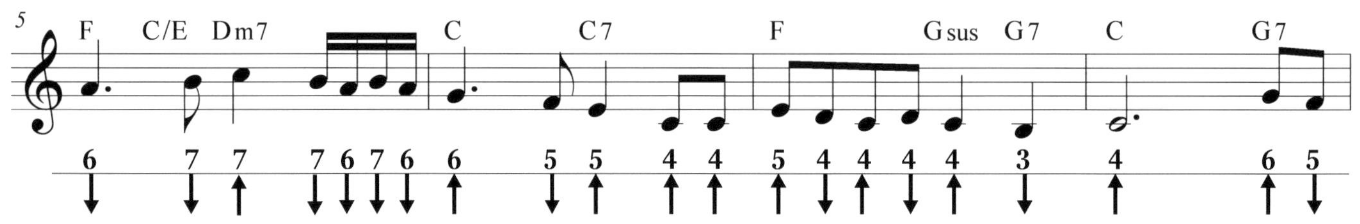

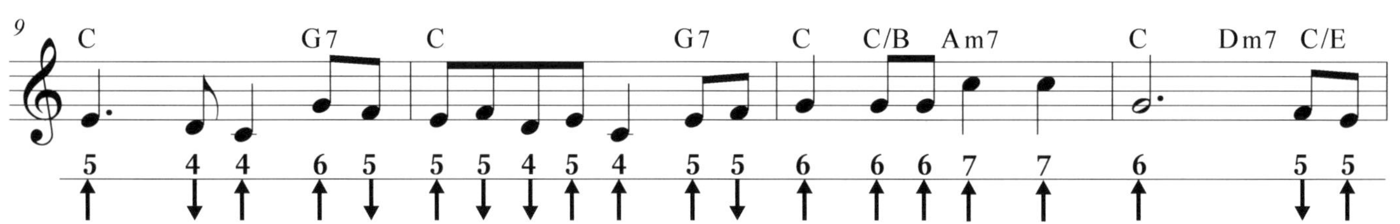

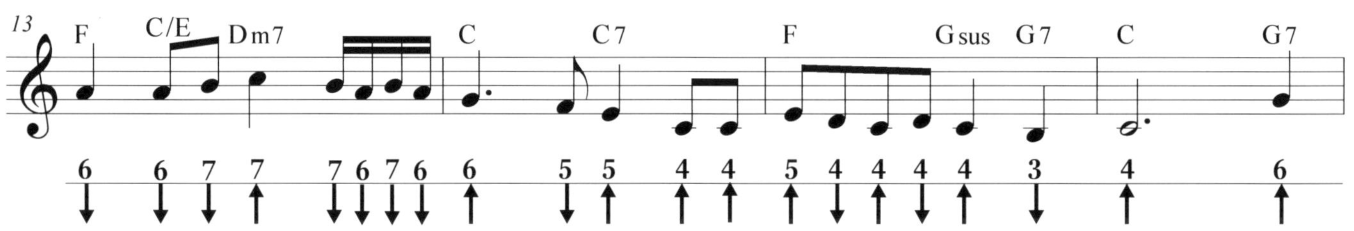

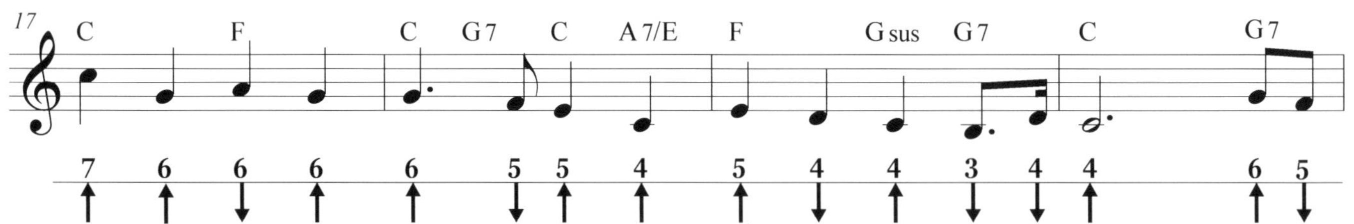

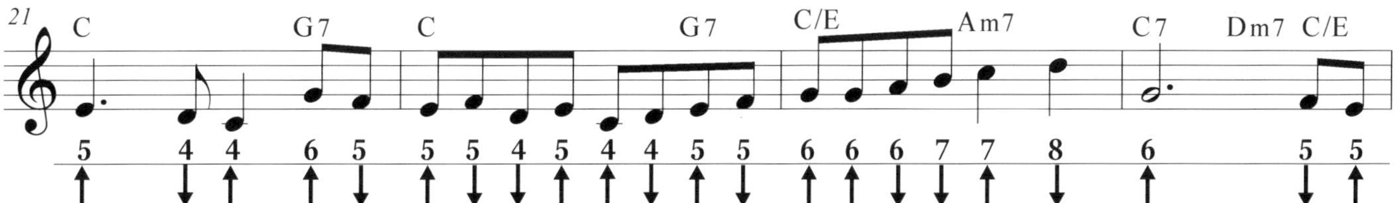
21
C G7 C G7 C/E Am7 C7 Dm7 C/E
5 4 4 6 5 5 5 4 5 4 4 5 5 6 6 6 7 7 8 6 5 5

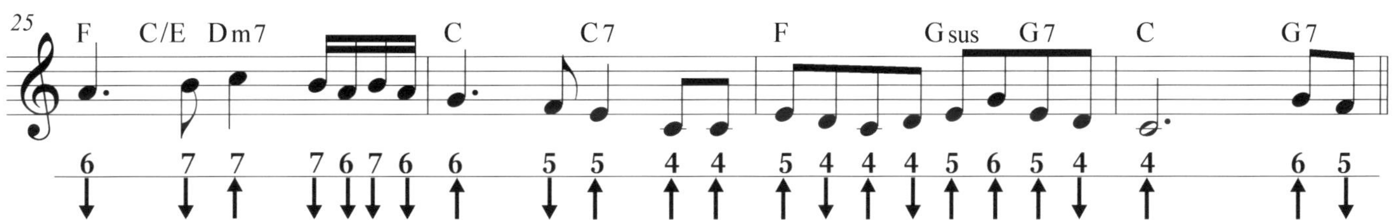
25
F C/E Dm7 C C7 F Gsus G7 C G7
6 7 7 7 6 7 6 6 5 5 4 4 5 4 4 4 5 6 5 4 4 6 5

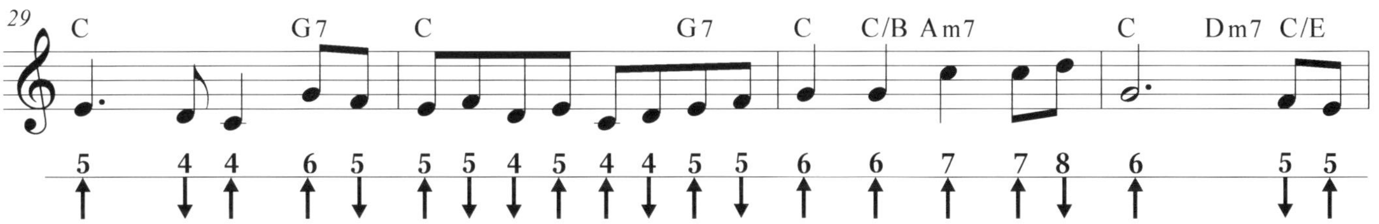
29
C G7 C G7 C C/B Am7 C Dm7 C/E
5 4 4 6 5 5 5 4 5 4 4 5 5 6 6 7 7 8 6 5 5

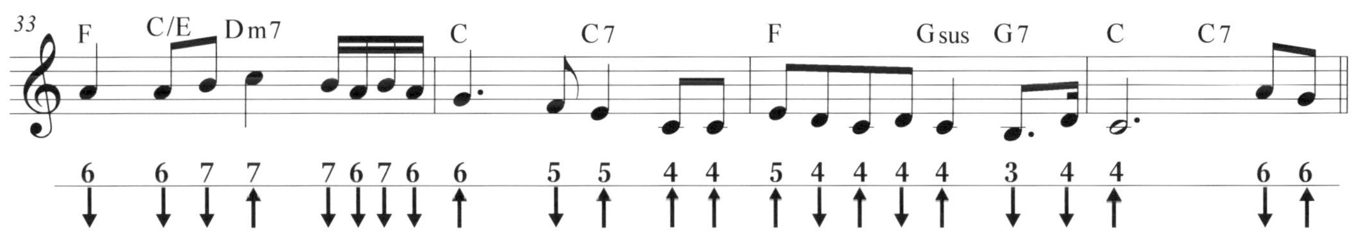
33
F C/E Dm7 C C7 F Gsus G7 C C7
6 6 7 7 7 6 7 6 6 5 5 4 4 5 4 4 4 4 3 4 4 6 6

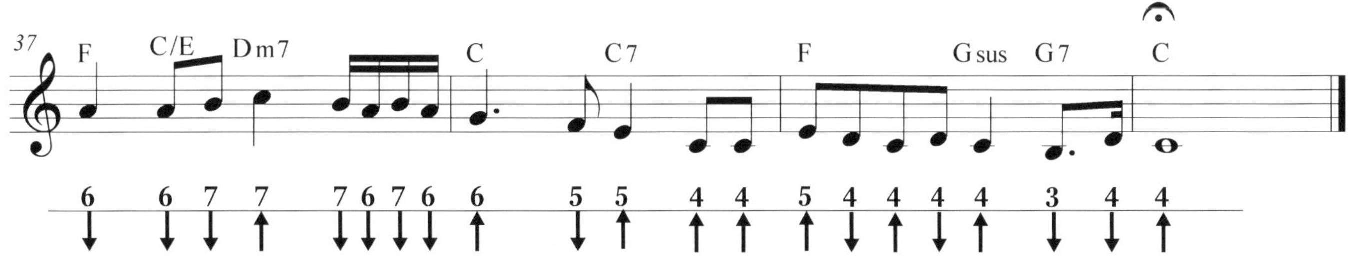
37
F C/E Dm7 C C7 F Gsus G7 C
6 6 7 7 7 6 7 6 6 5 5 4 4 5 4 4 4 4 3 4 4

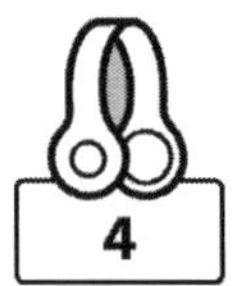

The Water Is Wide

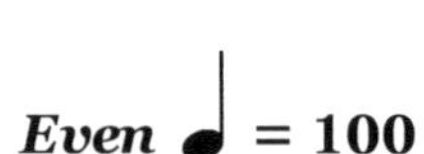

English Folk Song of Scottish Origin

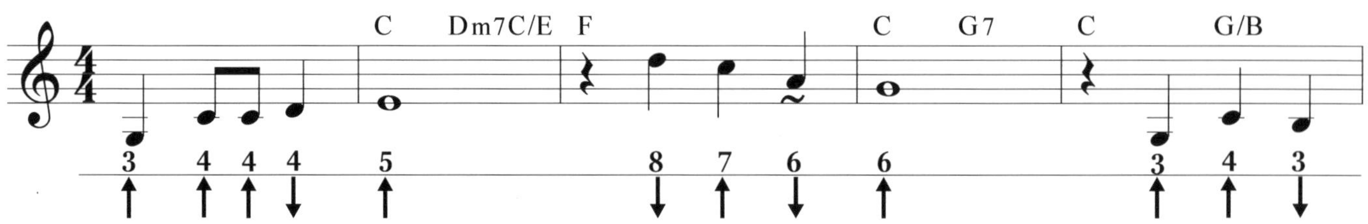

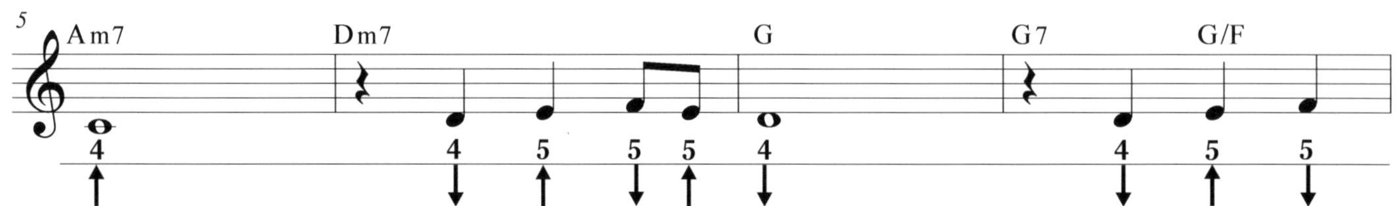

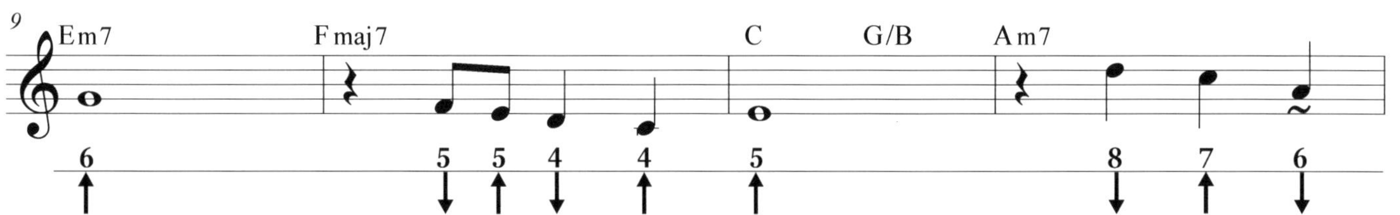

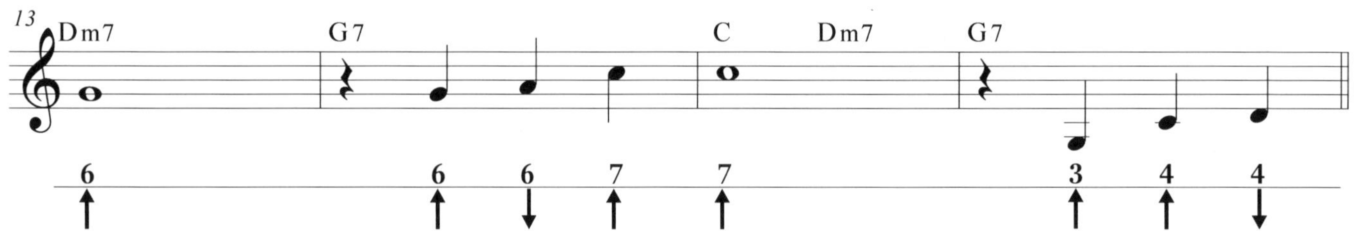

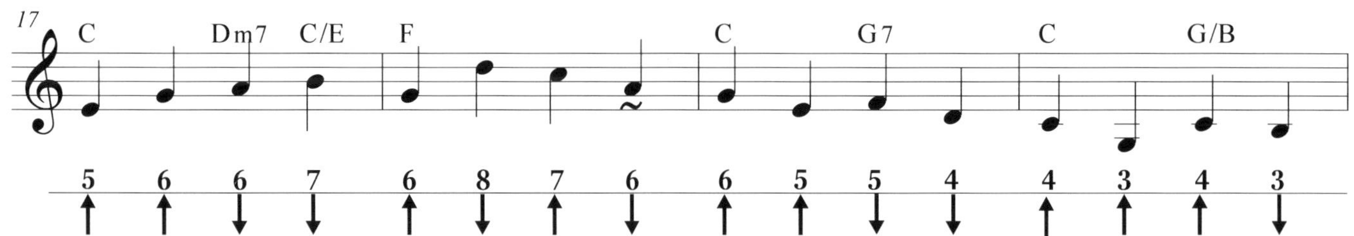

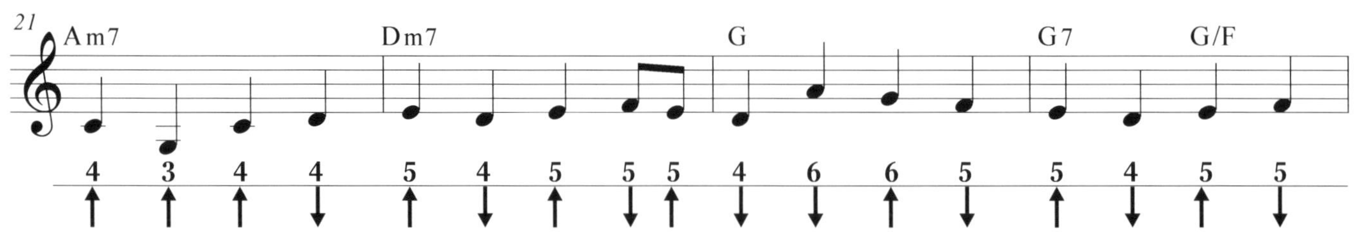

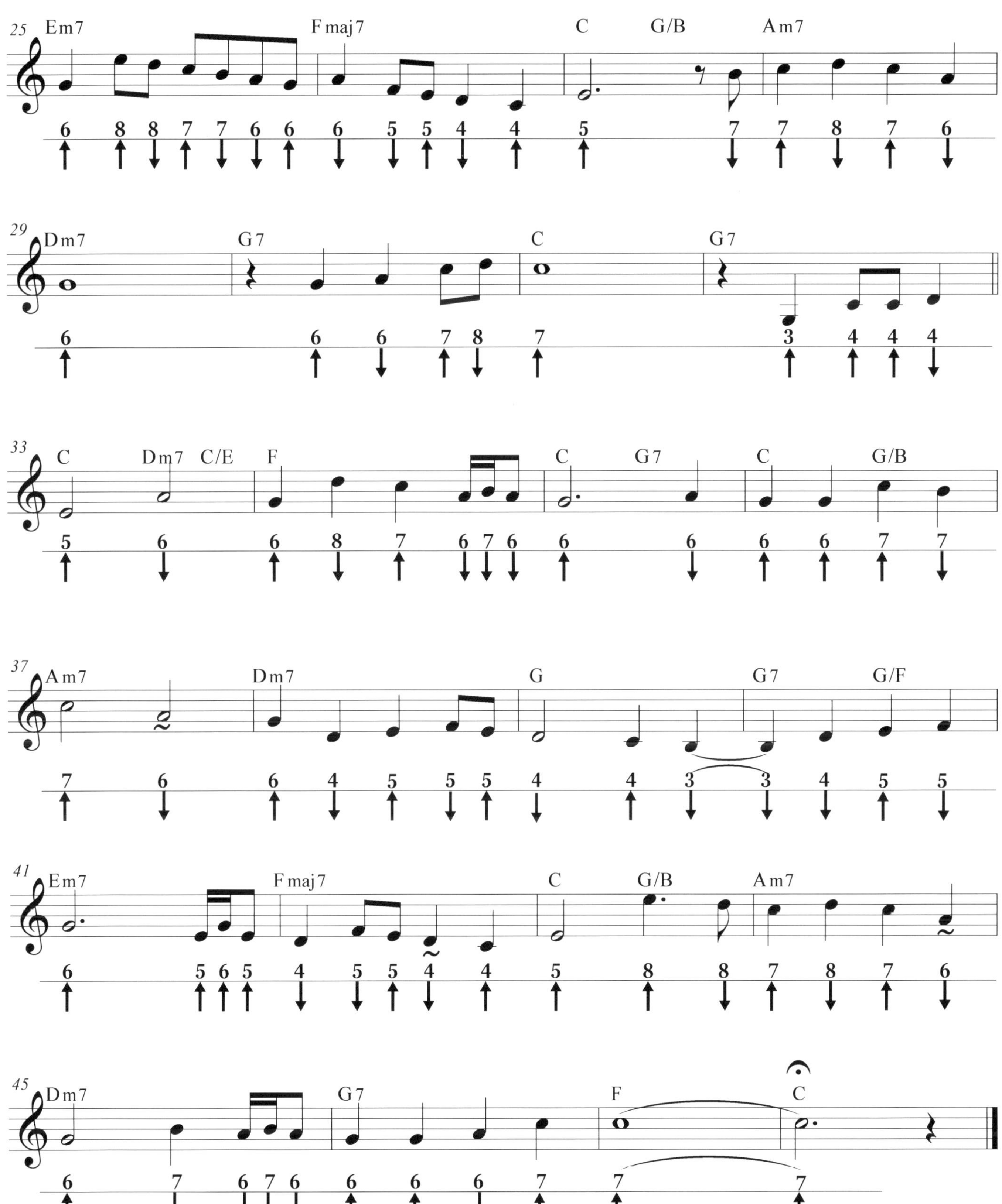
25 Em7 Fmaj7 C G/B Am7
6 8 8 7 7 6 6 6 5 5 4 4 5 7 7 8 7 6
29 Dm7 G7 C G7
6 6 6 7 8 7 3 4 4 4
33 C Dm7 C/E F C G7 C G/B
5 6 6 8 7 6 7 6 6 6 6 6 7 7
37 Am7 Dm7 G G7 G/F
7 6 6 4 5 5 5 4 4 3 3 4 5 5
41 Em7 Fmaj7 C G/B Am7
6 5 6 5 4 5 5 4 4 5 8 8 7 8 7 6
45 Dm7 G7 F C
6 7 6 7 6 6 6 6 7 7 7

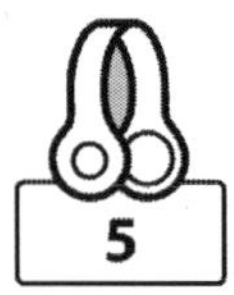

Scarborough Fair *(D Dorian)*

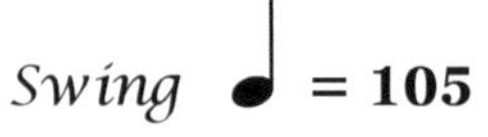

English ballad 14th Century

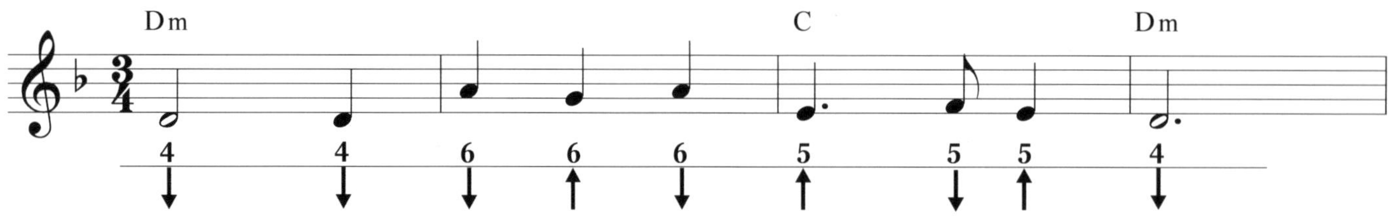

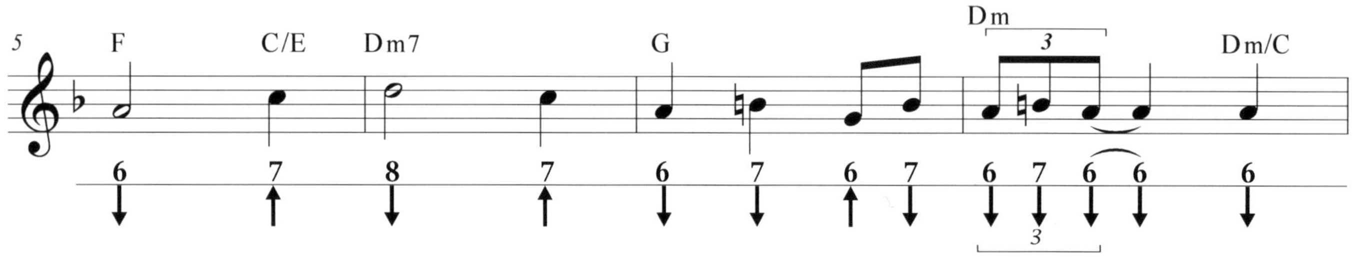

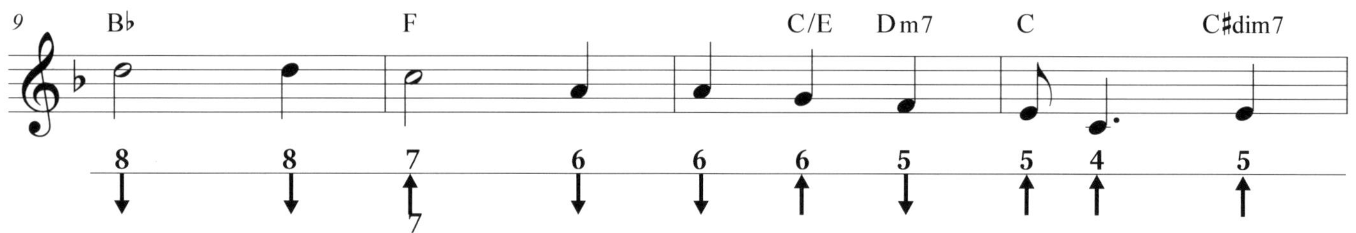

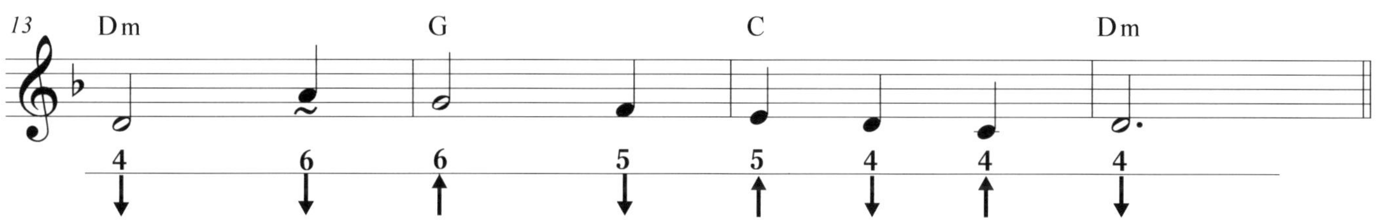

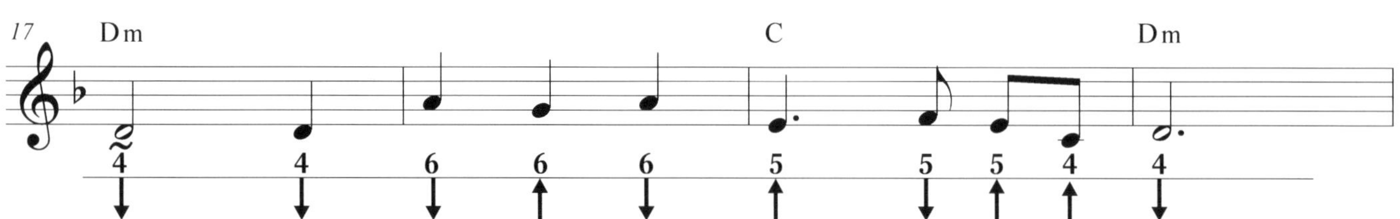

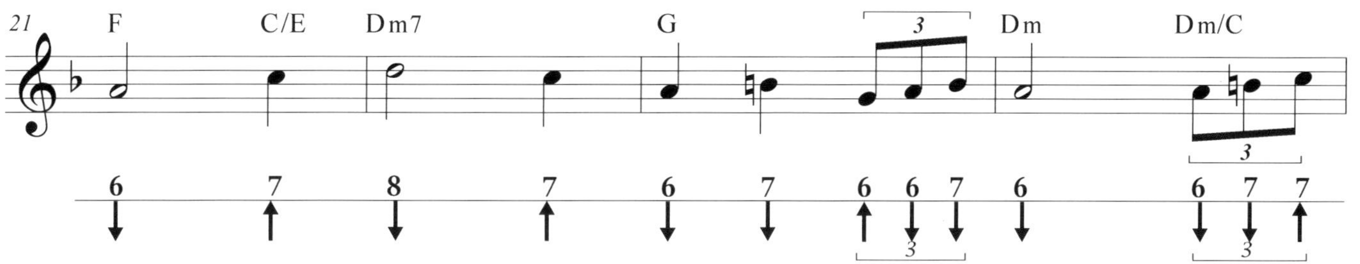
21
F C/E Dm7 G Dm Dm/C
3
3
6 7 8 7 6 7 6 6 7 6 6 7 7
3
3

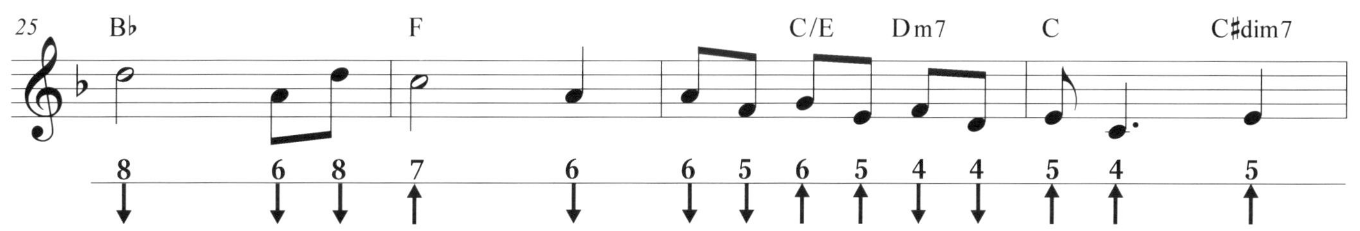
25
B♭ F C/E Dm7 C C♯dim7
8 6 8 7 6 6 5 6 5 4 4 5 4 5

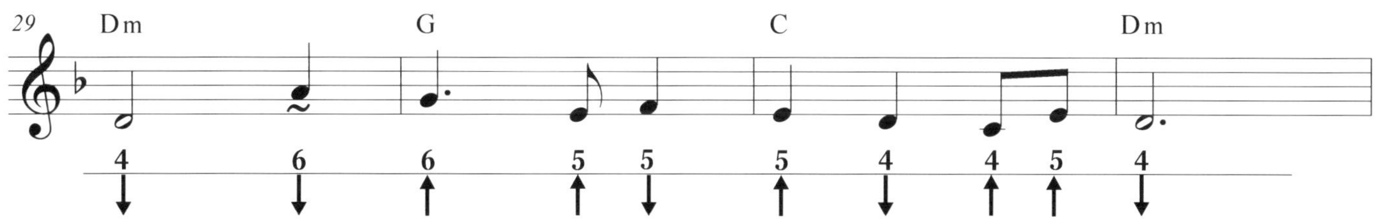
29
Dm G C Dm
4 6 6 5 5 5 4 4 5 4

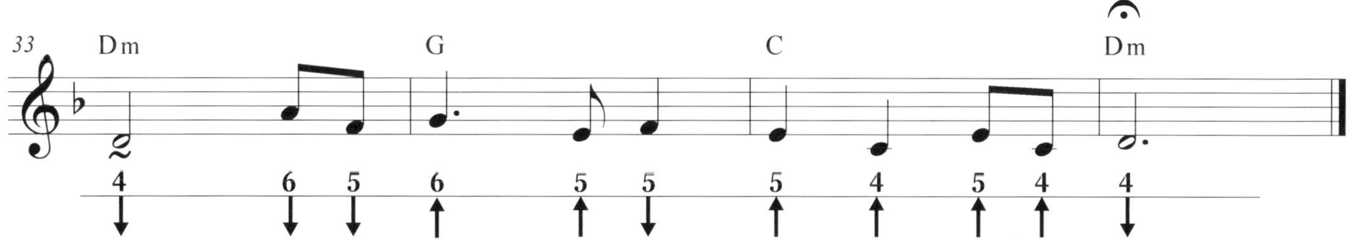
33
Dm G C Dm
4 6 5 6 5 5 5 4 5 4 4

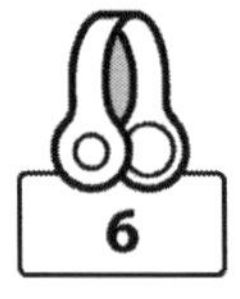

Drink to Me Only with Thine Eyes

♩ = 110

English

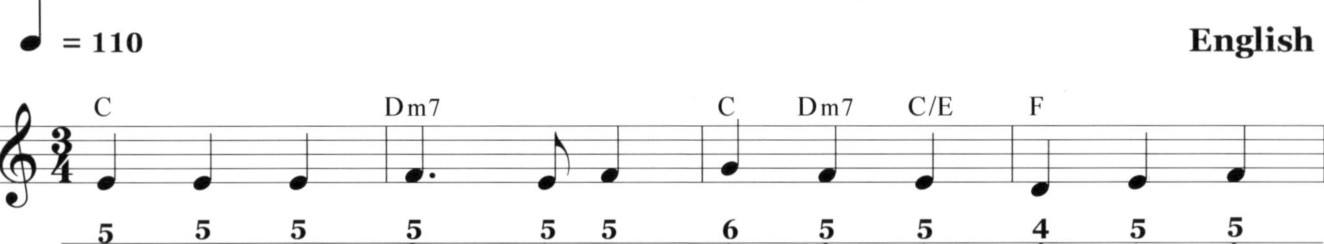

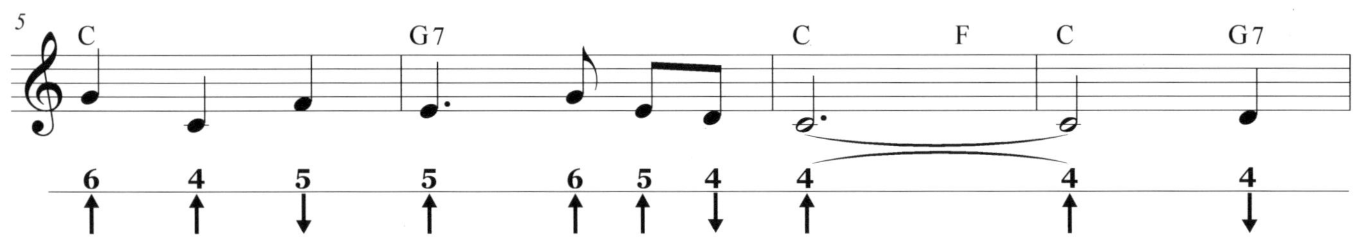

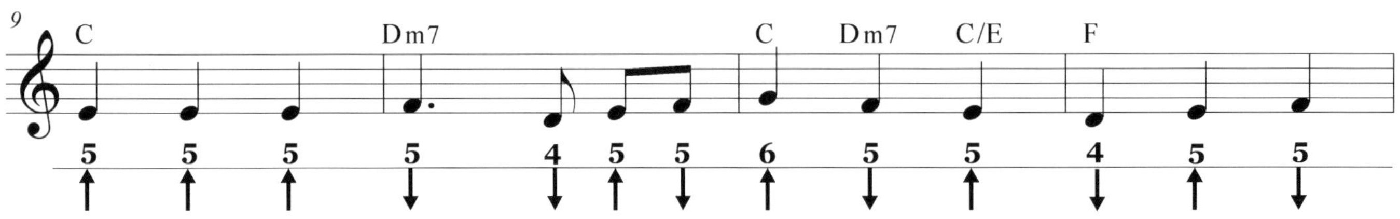

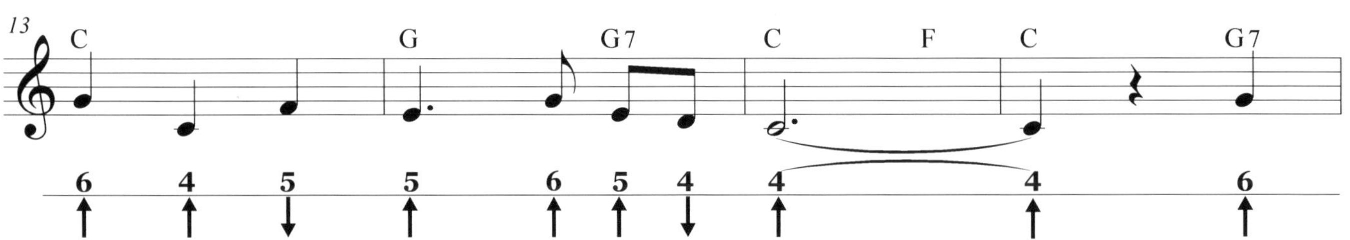

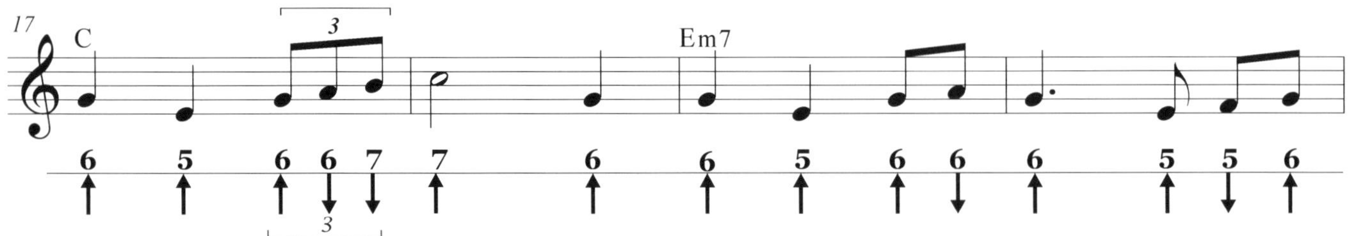

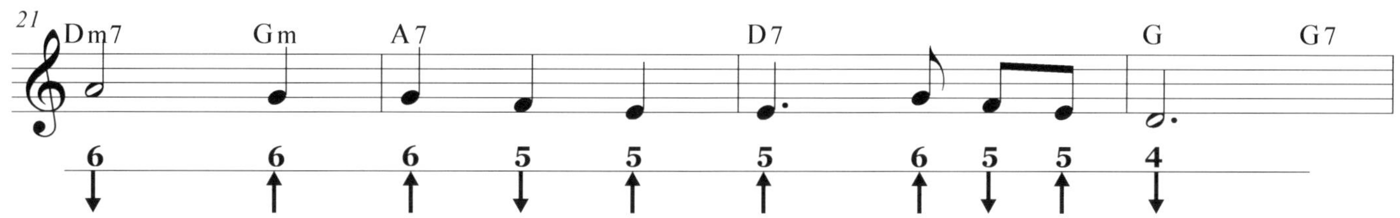
21
Dm7
Gm
A7
D7
G
G7
6 6 6 5 5 5 6 5 5 4

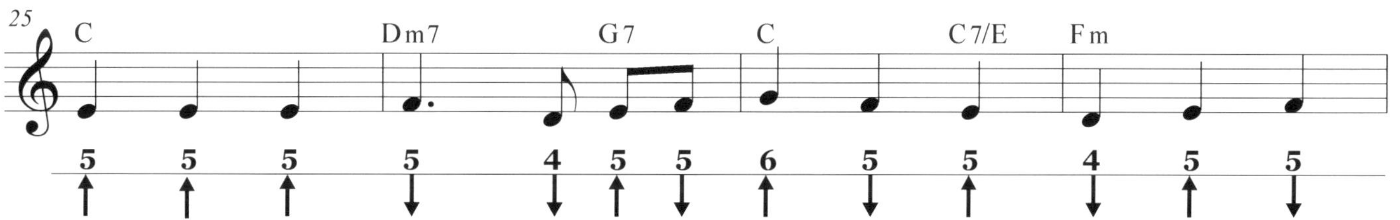
25
C
Dm7
G7
C
C7/E
Fm
5 5 5 5 4 5 5 6 5 5 4 5 5

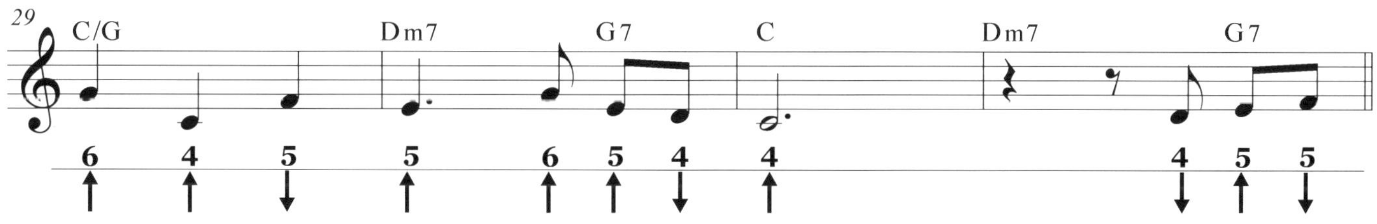
29
C/G
Dm7
G7
C
Dm7
G7
6 4 5 5 6 5 4 4 4 5 5

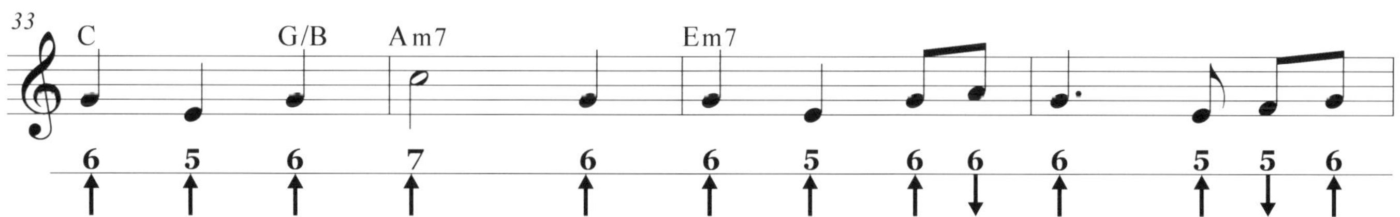
33
C
G/B
Am7
Em7
6 5 6 7 6 6 5 6 6 6 5 5 6

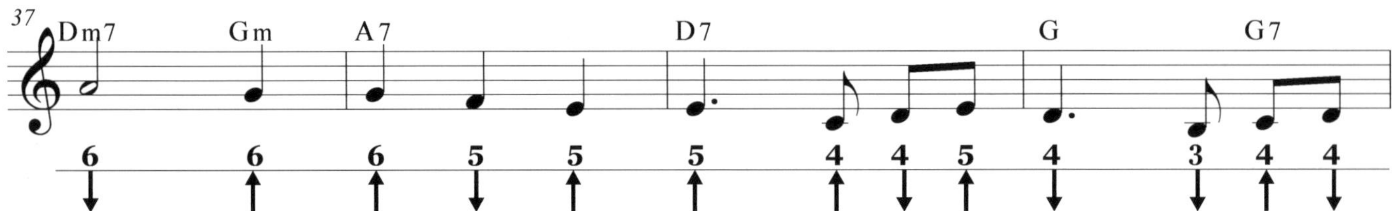
37
Dm7 Gm A7 D7 G G7
6 6 6 5 5 5 4 4 5 4 3 4 4

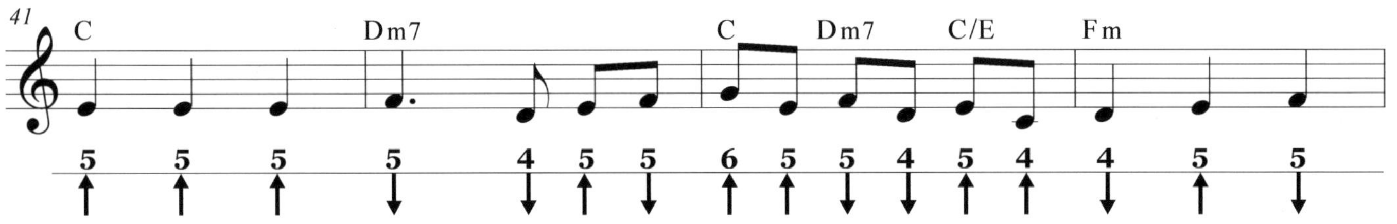
41
C Dm7 C Dm7 C/E Fm
5 5 5 5 4 5 5 6 5 5 4 5 4 4 5 5

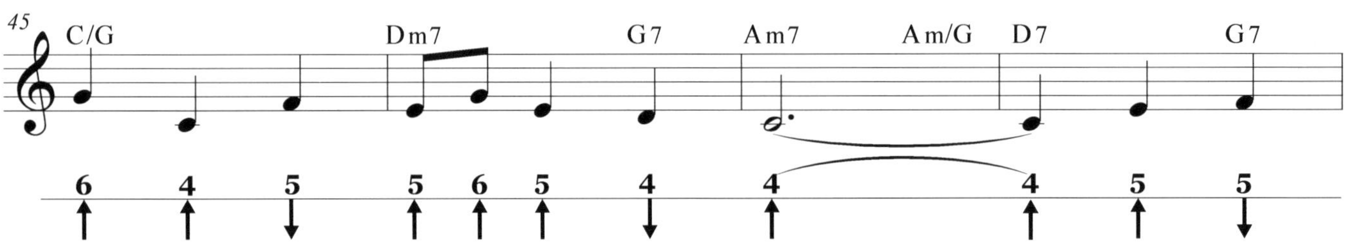
45
C/G Dm7 G7 Am7 Am/G D7 G7
6 4 5 5 6 5 4 4 4 5 5

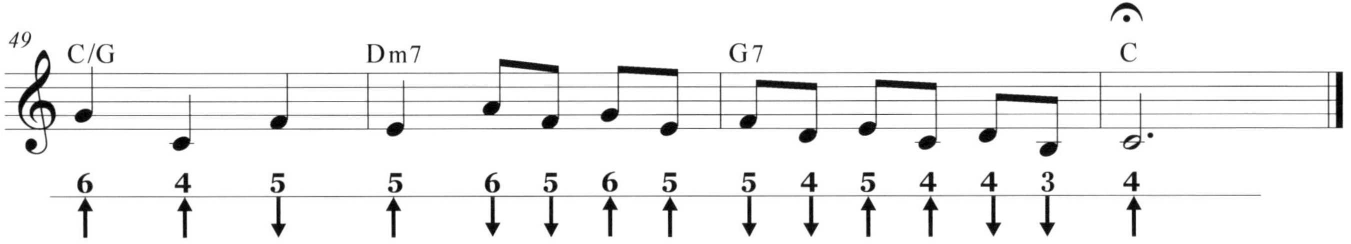
49
C/G Dm7 G7 C
6 4 5 5 6 5 6 5 5 4 5 4 4 3 4

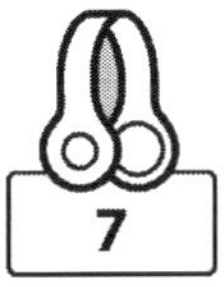

John Peel

Even ♩ **= 110**

England

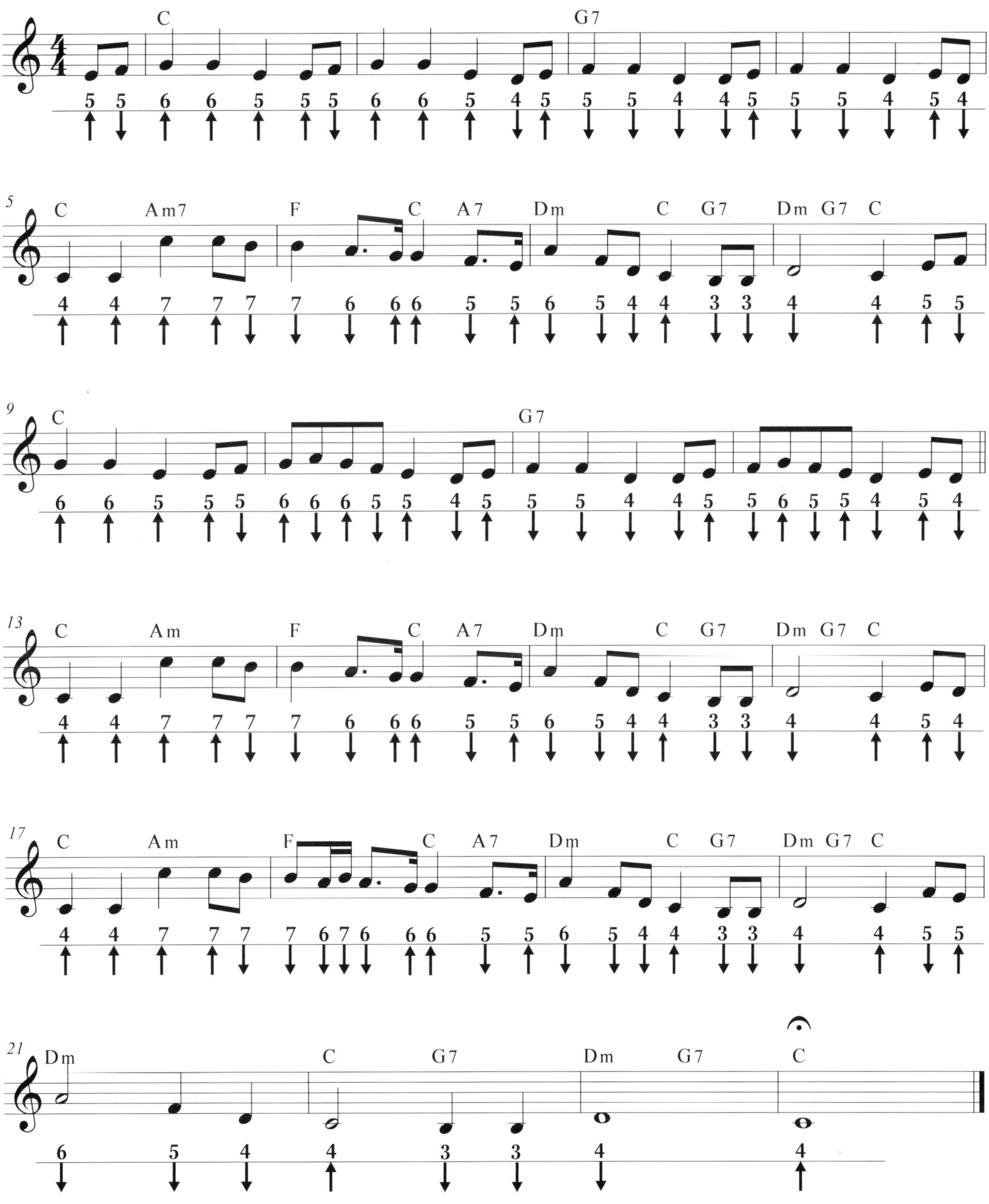

The Ash Grove

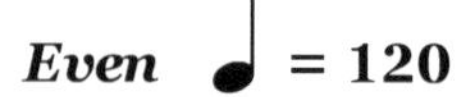

Welsh-Late 1600

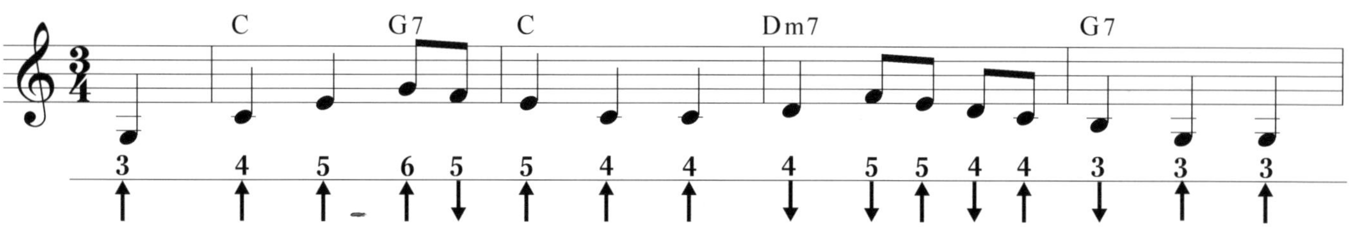

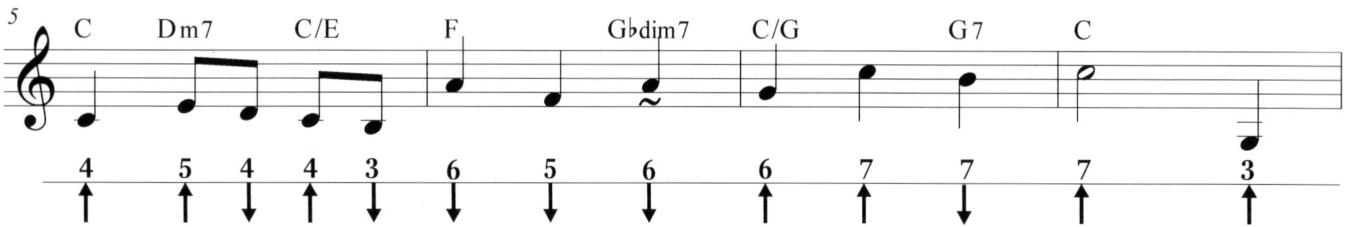

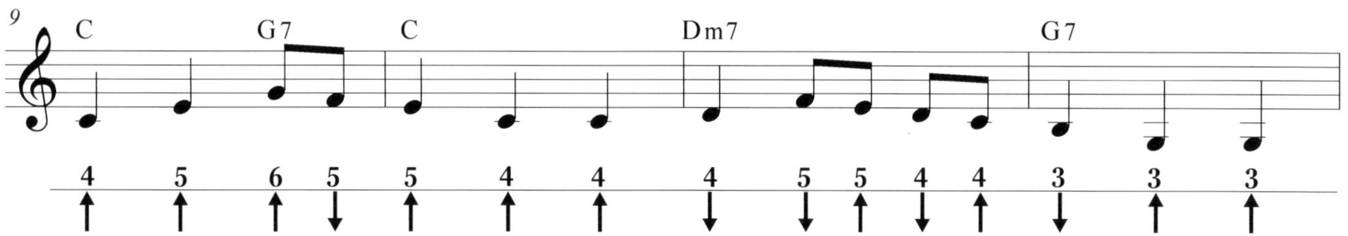

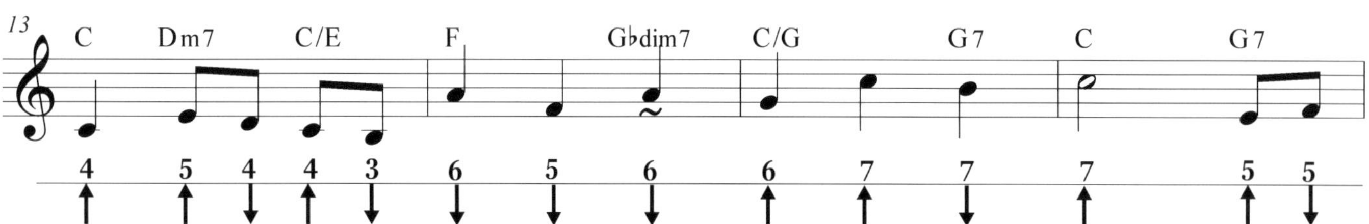

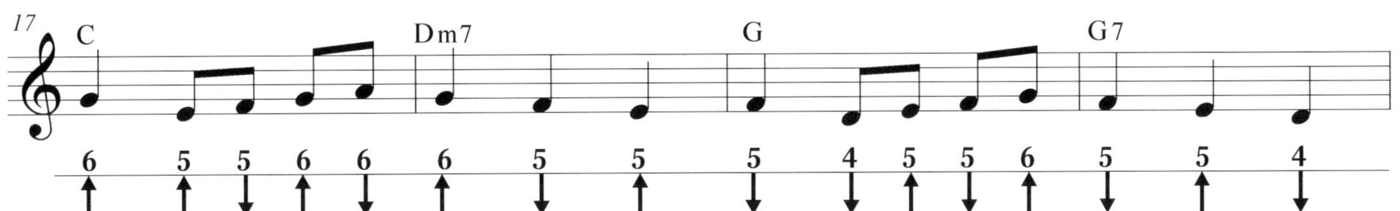
17
C
Dm7
G
G7
6 5 5 6 6 6 5 5 5 4 5 5 6 5 5 4

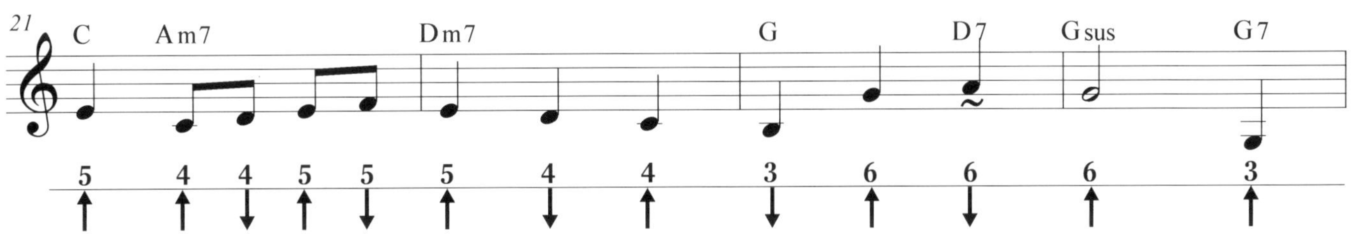
21
C
Am7
Dm7
G
D7
Gsus
G7
5 4 4 5 5 5 4 4 3 6 6 6 3

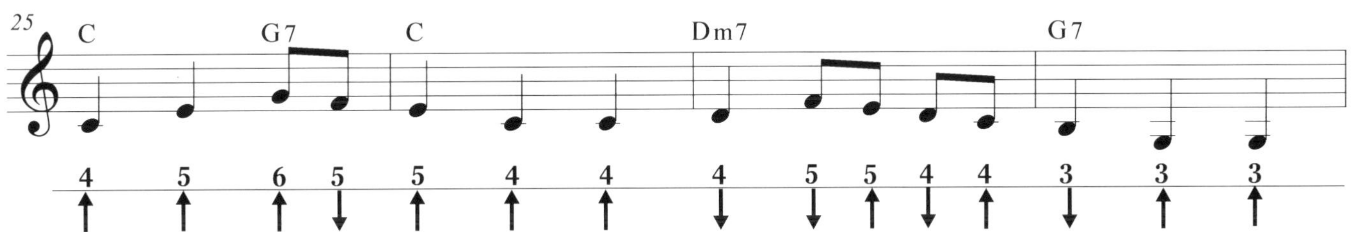
25
C
G7
C
Dm7
G7
4 5 6 5 5 4 4 4 5 5 4 4 3 3 3

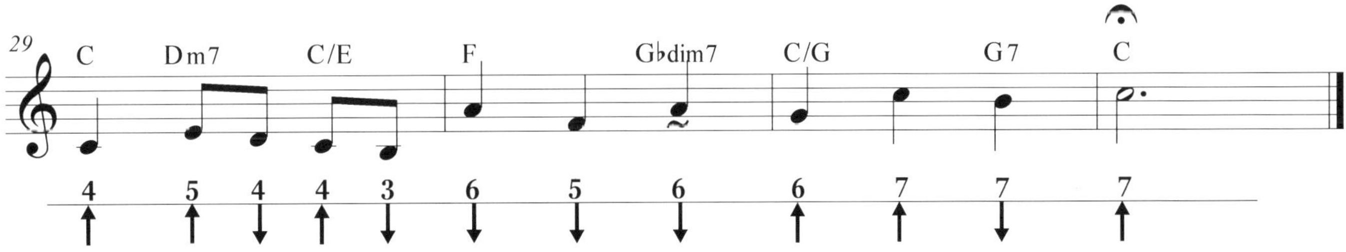
29
C
Dm7
C/E
F
G♭dim7
C/G
G7
C
4 5 4 4 3 6 5 6 6 7 7 7

I Gave My Love a Cherry

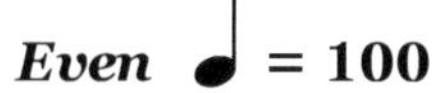

English 15th Century

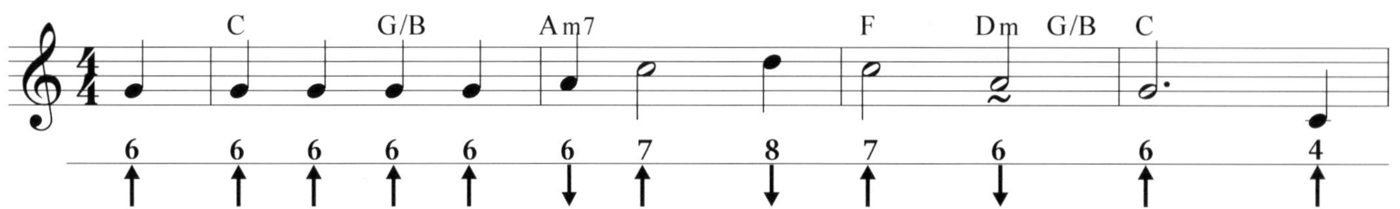

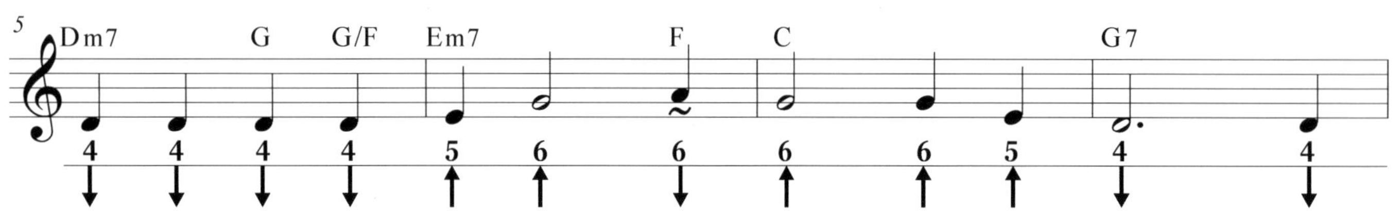

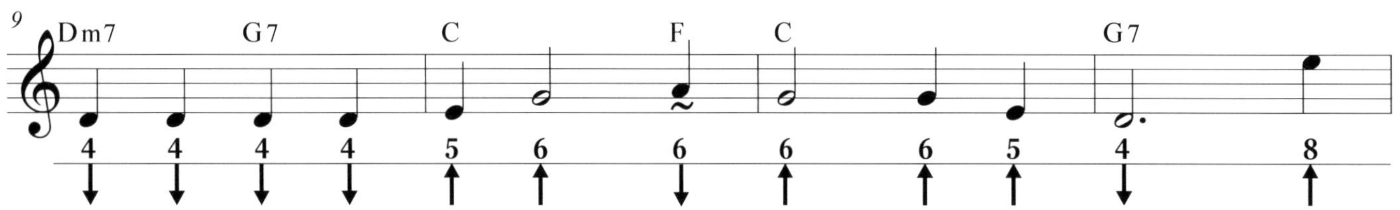

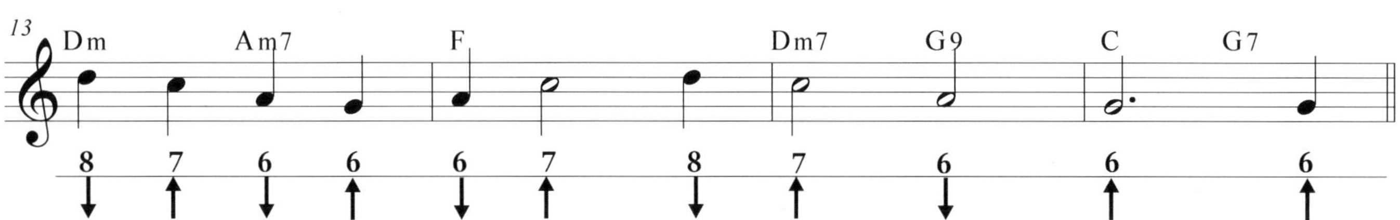

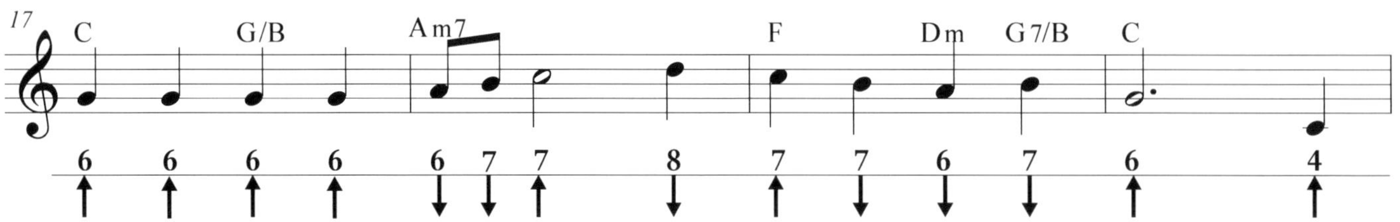

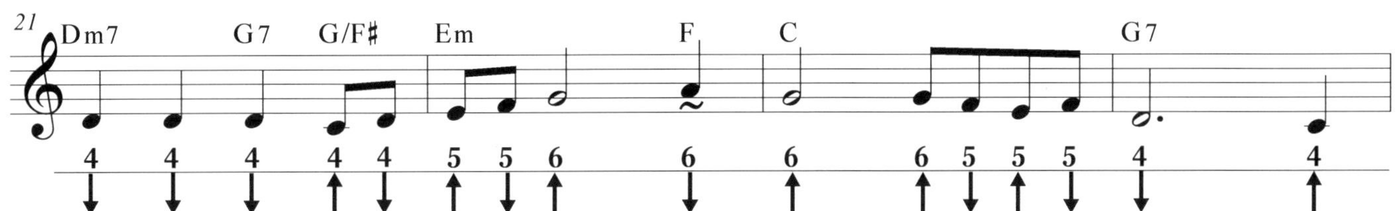
21
Dm7 G7 G/F♯ Em F C G7
4 4 4 4 4 5 5 6 6 6 6 5 5 5 4 4

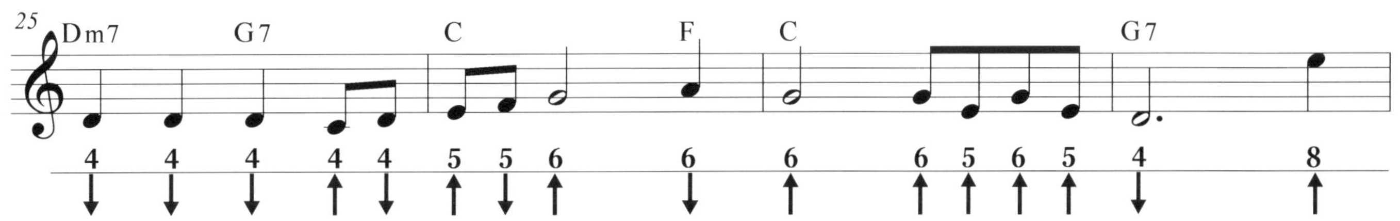
25
Dm7 G7 C F C G7
4 4 4 4 4 5 5 6 6 6 6 5 6 5 4 8

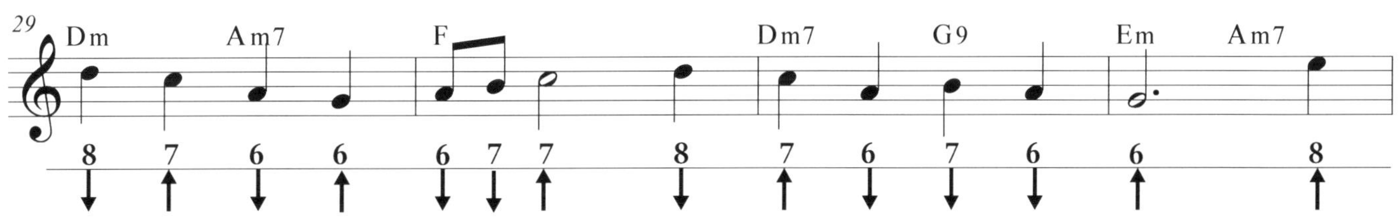
29
Dm Am7 F Dm7 G9 Em Am7
8 7 6 6 6 7 7 8 7 6 7 6 6 8

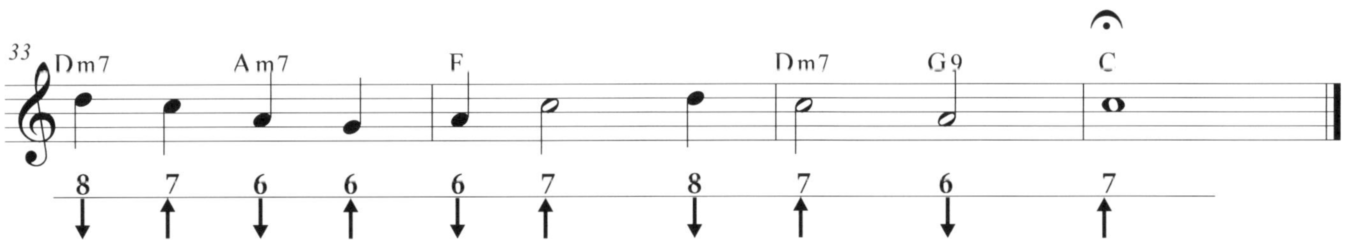
33
Dm7 Am7 F Dm7 G9 C
8 7 6 6 6 7 8 7 6 7

The Gentle Maiden

Swing ♩ **= 95** *Gentle flowing* **Irish Waltz Air**

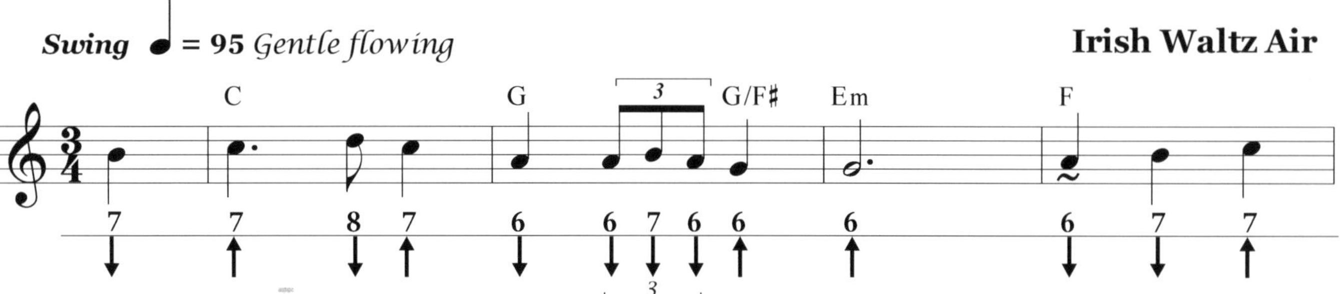

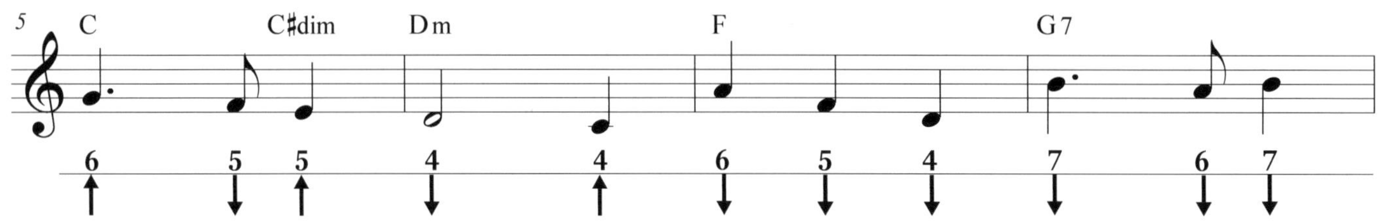

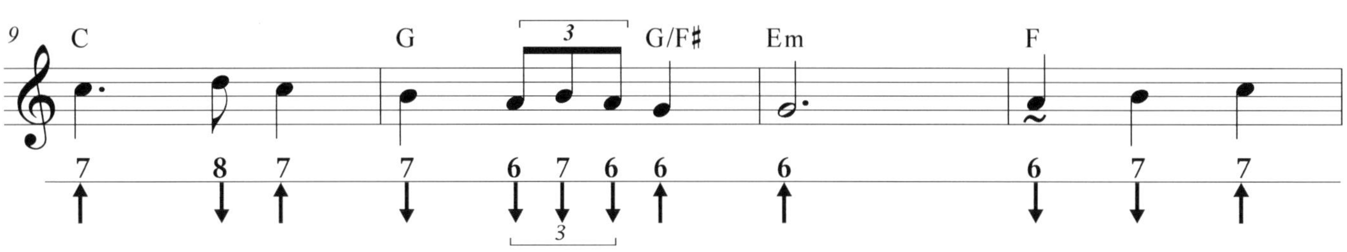

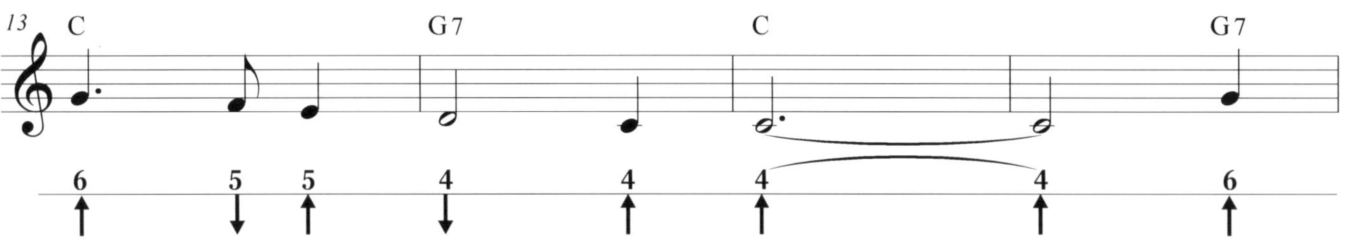

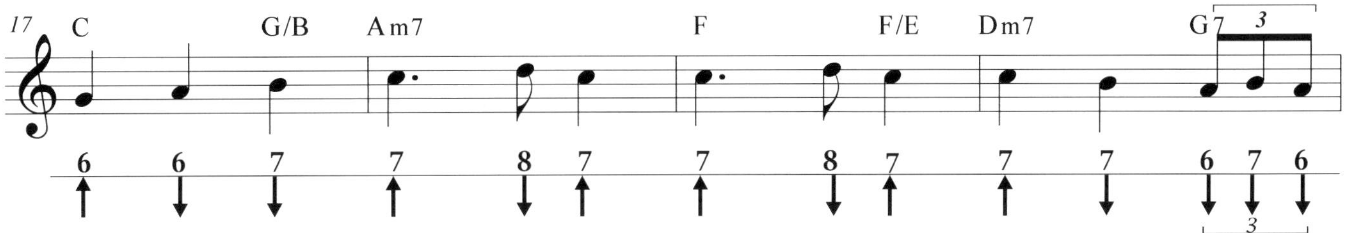
17
C G/B Am7 F F/E Dm7 G7

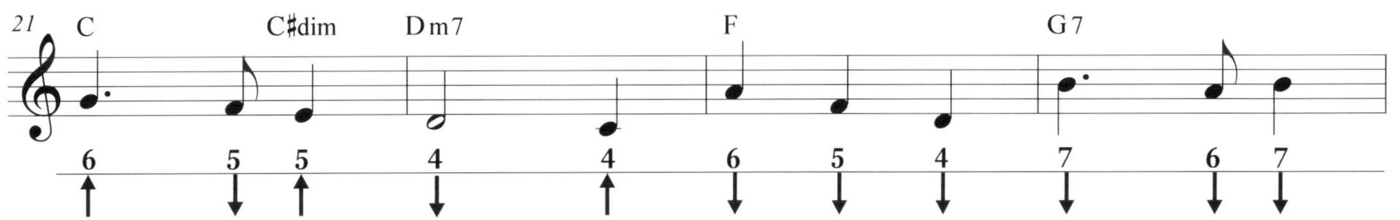
21
C C♯dim Dm7 F G7

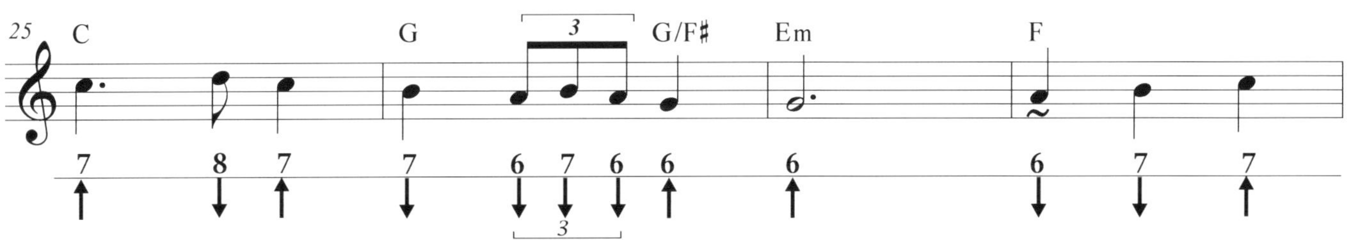
25
C G G/F♯ Em F

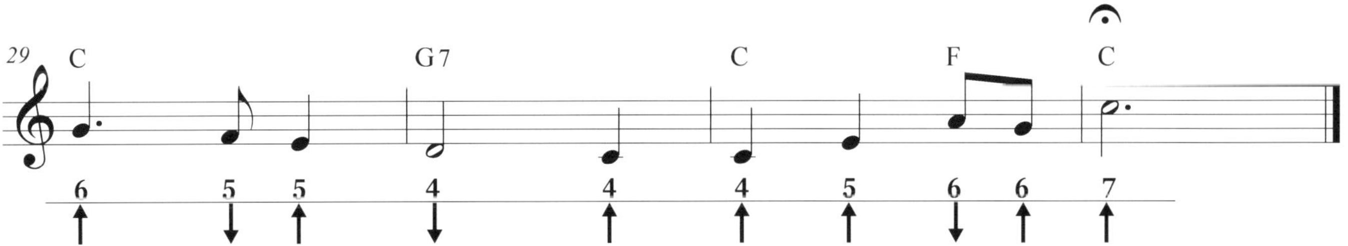
29
C G7 C F C

Hector the Hero (Scottish)

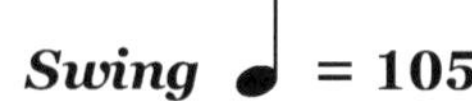

James Scott Skinner 1903

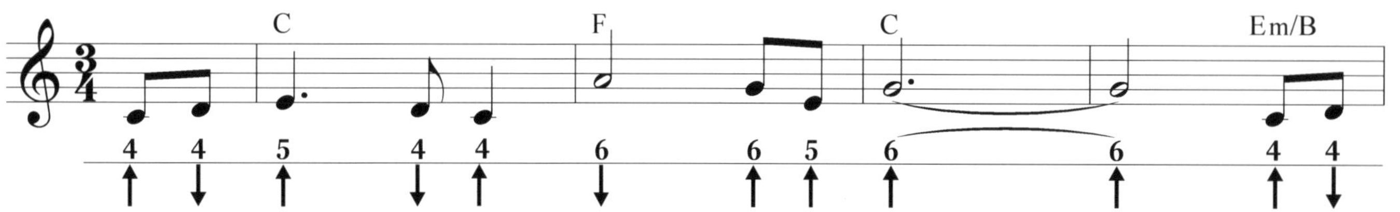

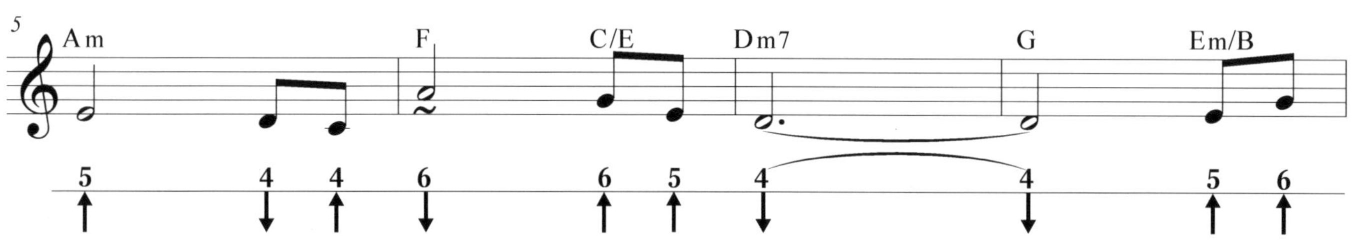

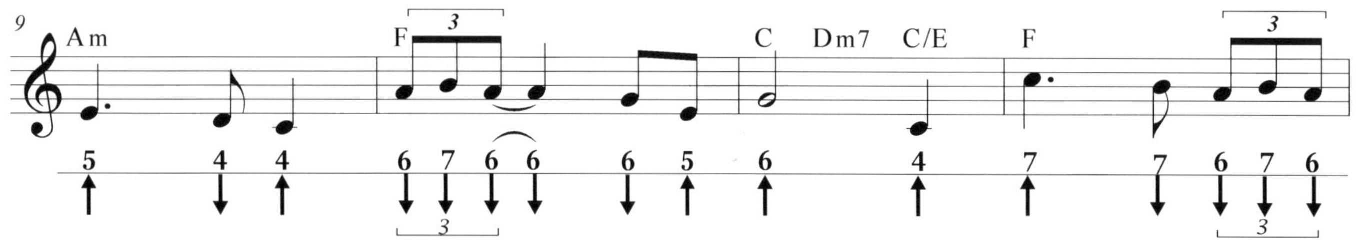

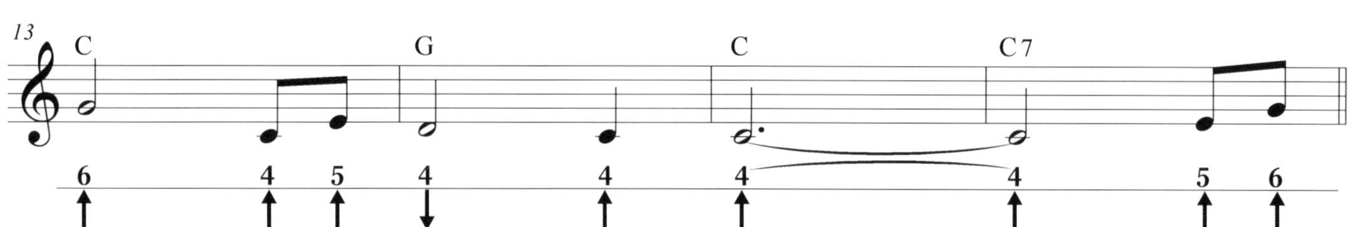

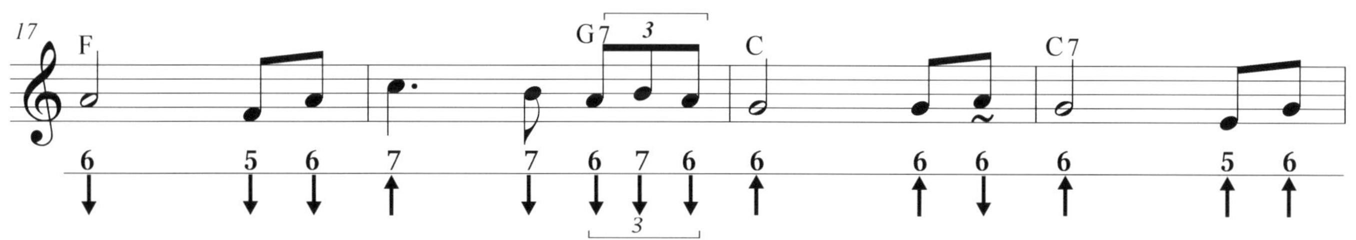

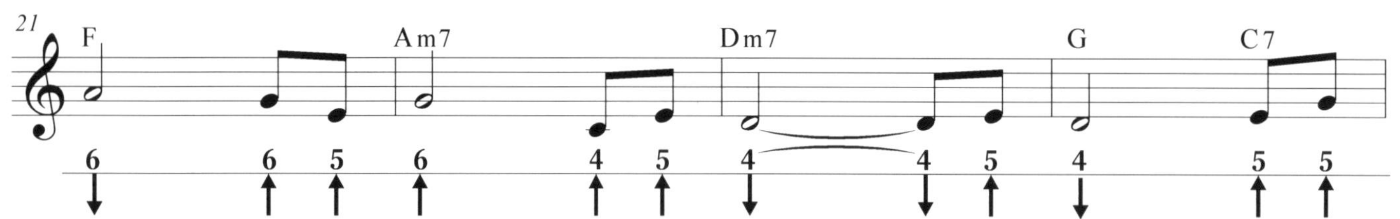

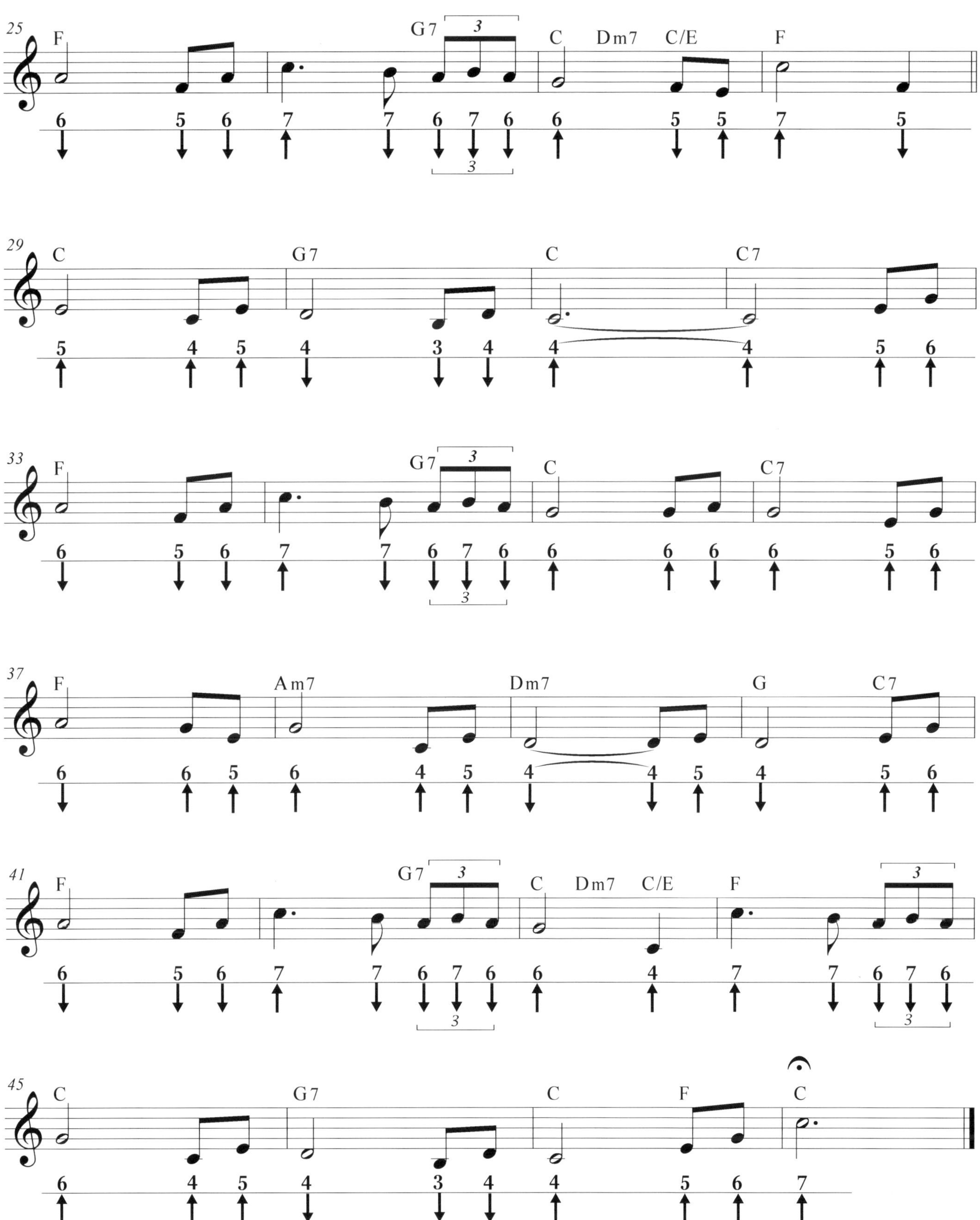
25
F
G7
3
C
Dm7
C/E
F
6 5 6 7 7 6 7 6 6 5 5 7 5
3
29
C
G7
C
C7
5 4 5 4 3 4 4 4 5 6
33
F
G7
3
C
C7
6 5 6 7 7 6 7 6 6 6 6 6 5 6
3
37
F
Am7
Dm7
G
C7
6 6 5 6 4 5 4 4 5 4 5 6
41
F
G7
3
C
Dm7
C/E
F
3
6 5 6 7 7 6 7 6 6 4 7 7 6 7 6
3
3
45
C
G7
C
F
C
6 4 5 4 3 4 4 5 6 7

The Star of the County Down *(D Dorian)*

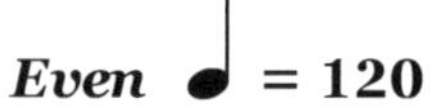

Northern Ireland Ballad

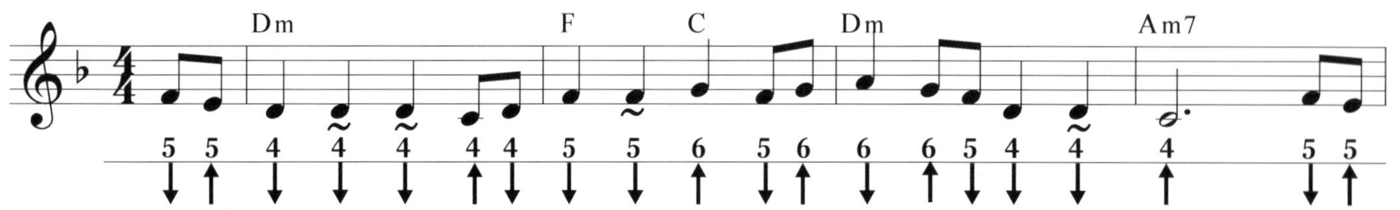

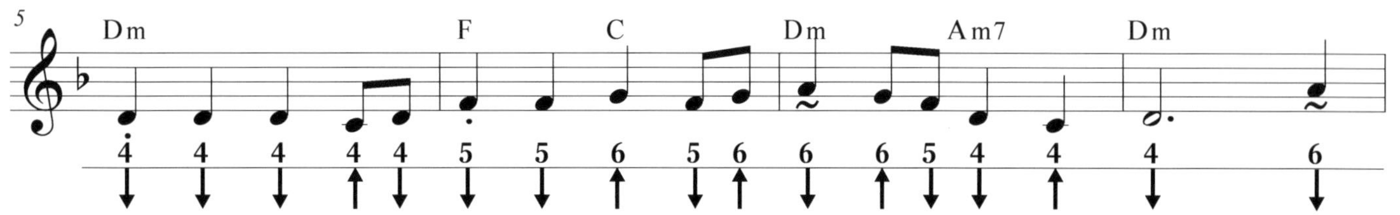

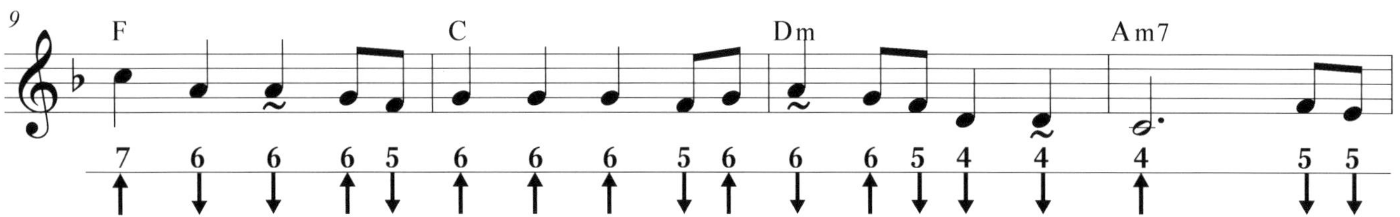

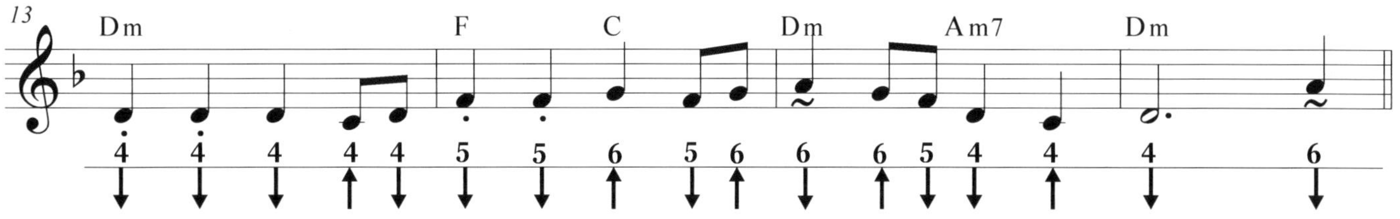

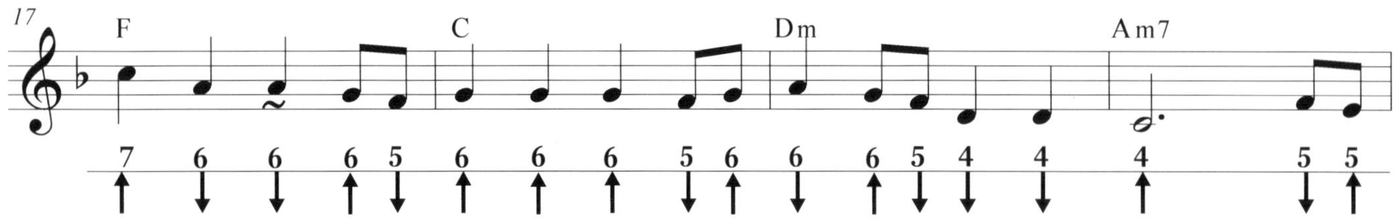

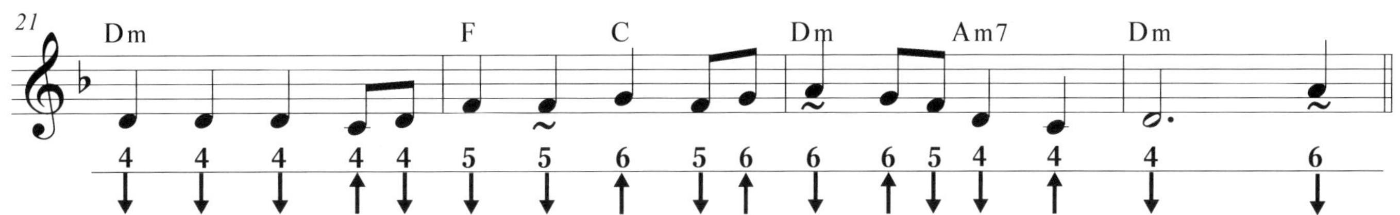
21
Dm F C Dm Am7 Dm
4 4 4 4 4 5 5 6 5 6 6 6 5 4 4 4 6

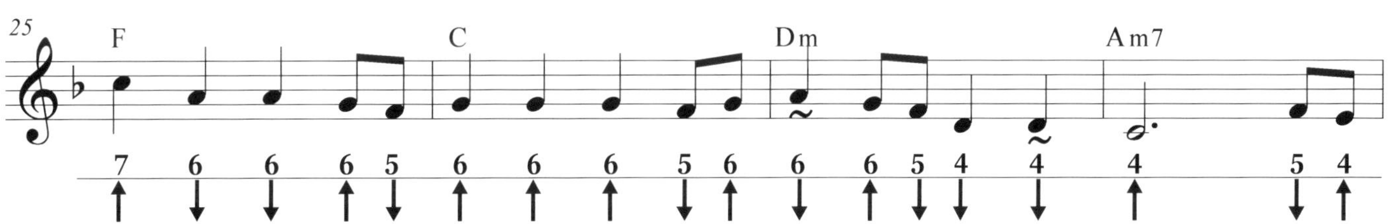
25
F C Dm Am7
7 6 6 6 5 6 6 6 5 6 6 6 5 4 4 4 5 4

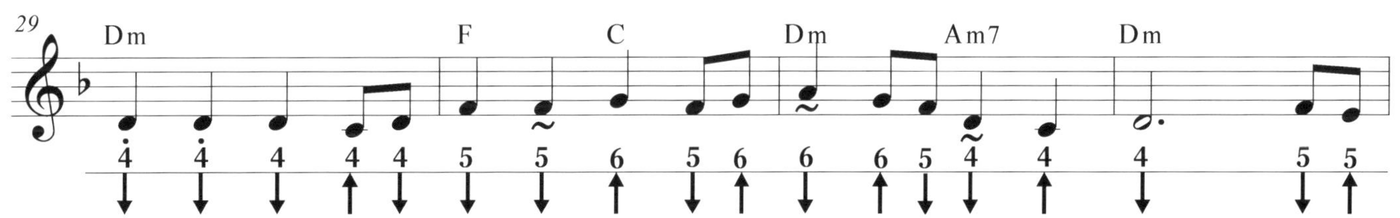
29
Dm F C Dm Am7 Dm
4 4 4 4 4 5 5 6 5 6 6 6 5 4 4 4 5 5

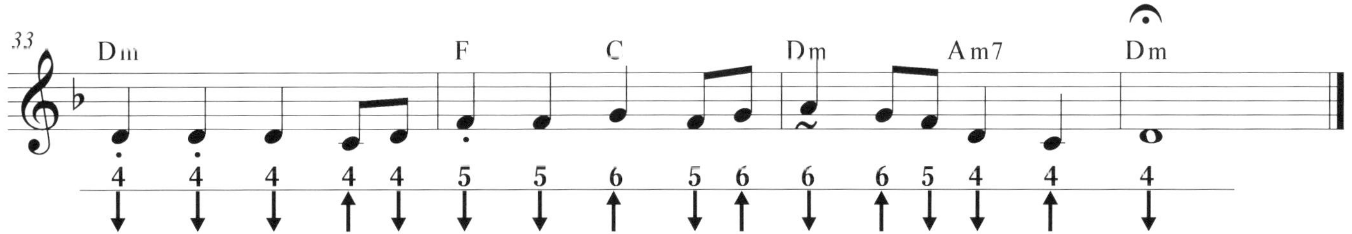
33
Dm F C Dm Am7 Dm
4 4 4 4 4 5 5 6 5 6 6 6 5 4 4 4

Sweet and Low

Even ♩ **= 110**

British

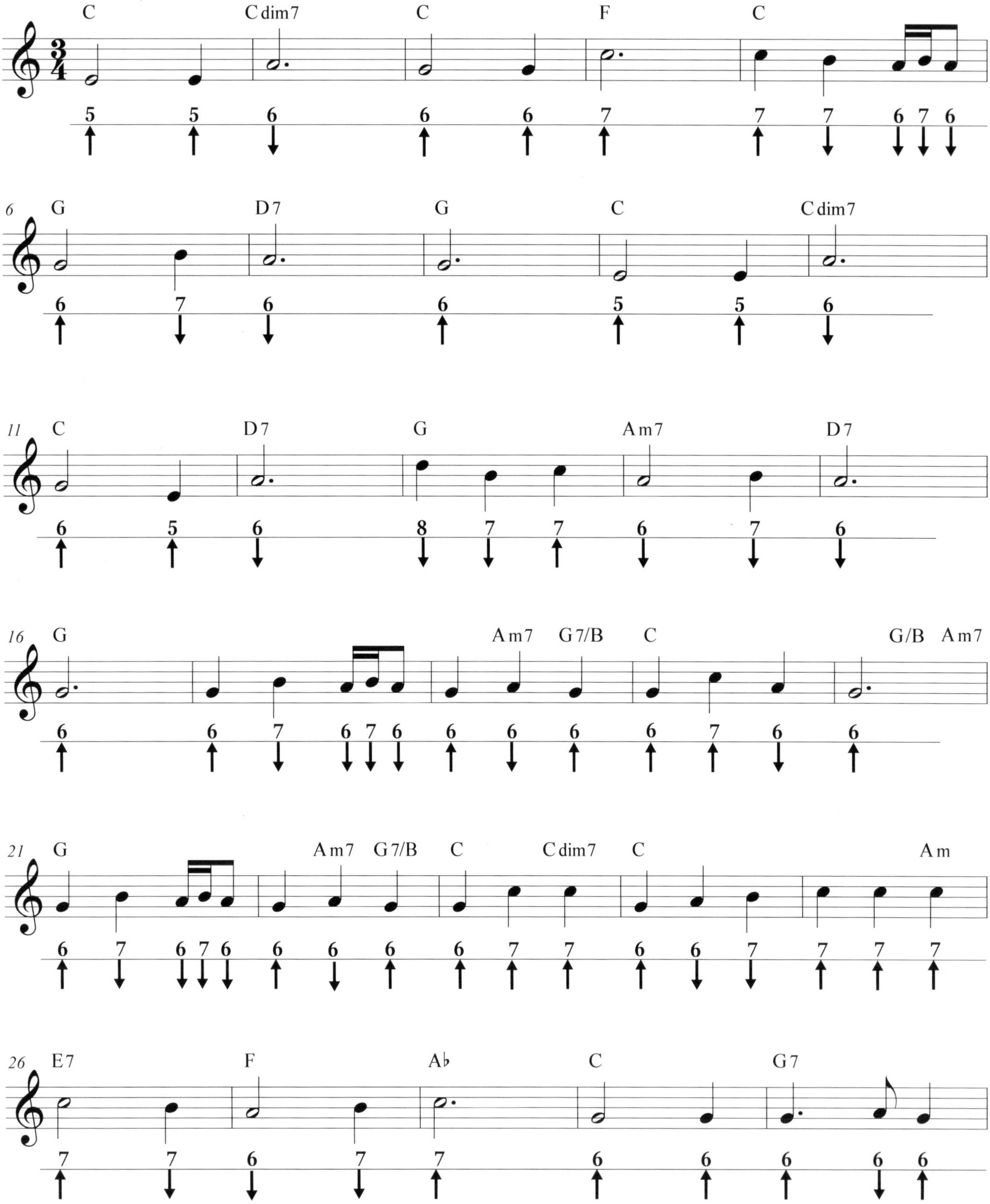

C C dim7 C F C

5↑ 5↑ 6↓ 6↑ 6↑ 7↑ 7↑ 7↓ 6↓ 7↓ 6↓

6 G D7 G C C dim7

6↑ 7↓ 6↓ 6↑ 5↑ 5↑ 6↓

11 C D7 G Am7 D7

6↑ 5↑ 6↓ 8↓ 7↓ 7↑ 6↓ 7↓ 6↓

16 G Am7 G7/B C G/B Am7

6↑ 6↑ 7↓ 6↓ 7↓ 6↓ 6↑ 6↓ 6↑ 6↑ 7↑ 6↓ 6↑

21 G Am7 G7/B C C dim7 C Am

6↑ 7↓ 6↓ 7↓ 6↓ 6↑ 6↓ 6↑ 6↑ 7↑ 7↑ 6↑ 6↓ 7↓ 7↑ 7↑ 7↑

26 E7 F A♭ C G7

7↑ 7↓ 6↓ 7↓ 7↑ 6↑ 6↑ 6↑ 6↓ 6↑

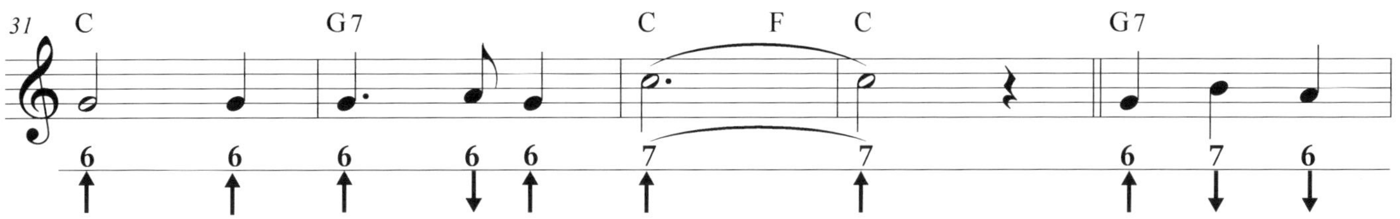
31
C G7 C F C G7
6 6 6 6 6 7 7 6 7 6

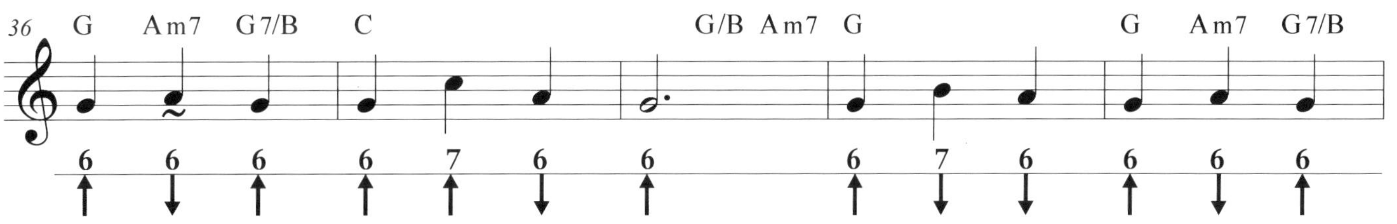
36
G Am7 G7/B C G/B Am7 G G Am7 G7/B
6 6 6 6 7 6 6 6 7 6 6 6 6

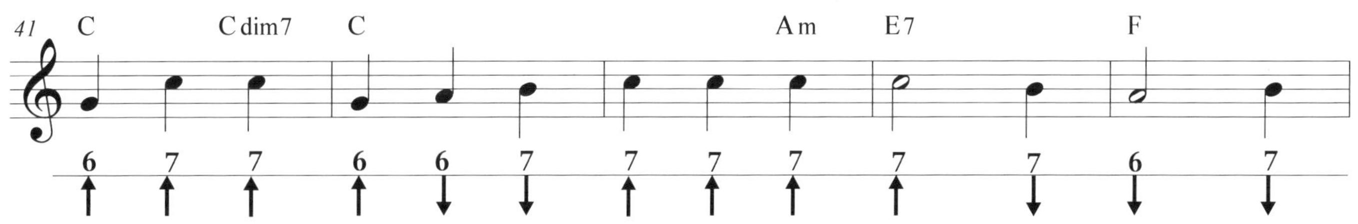
41
C Cdim7 C Am E7 F
6 7 7 6 6 7 7 7 7 7 7 6 7

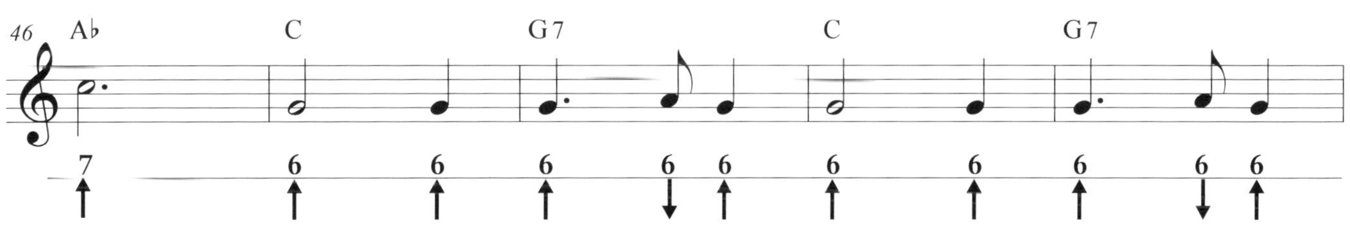
46
A♭ C G7 C G7
7 6 6 6 6 6 6 6 6 6 6

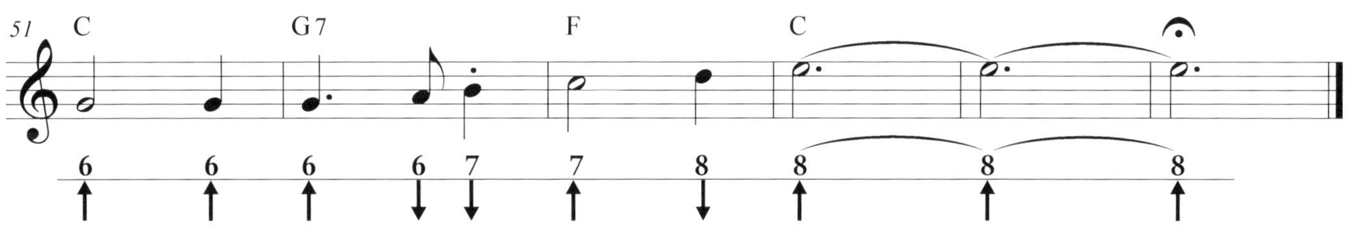
51
C G7 F C
6 6 6 6 7 7 8 8 8 8

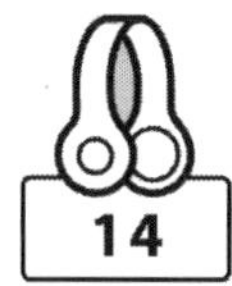

Two Maids Went A-Milking One Day

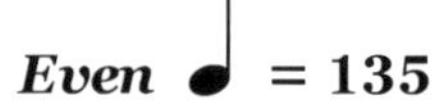

English Folk 17th Century

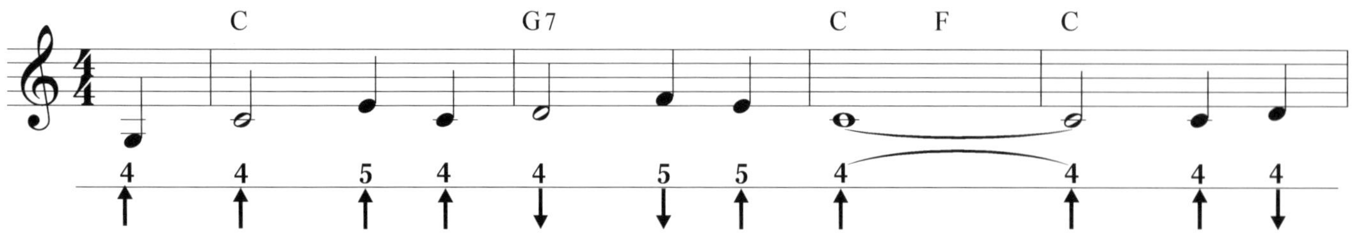

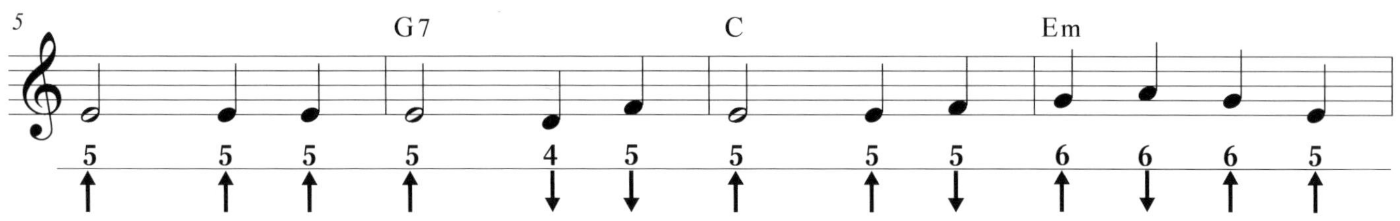

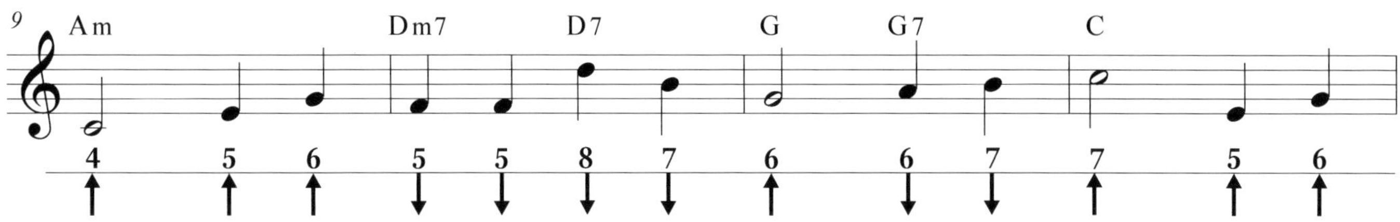

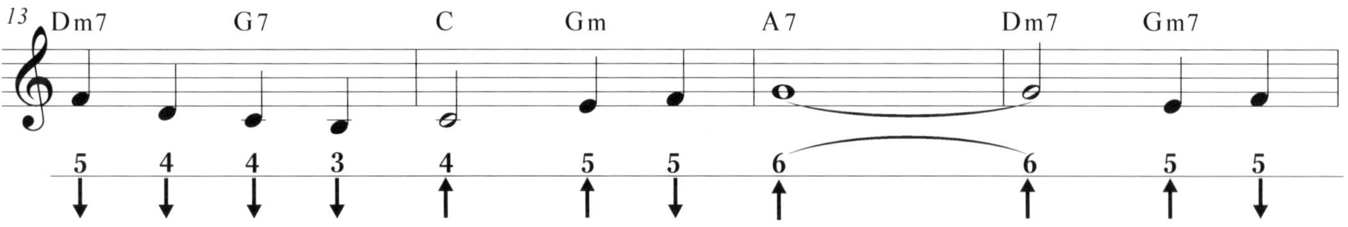

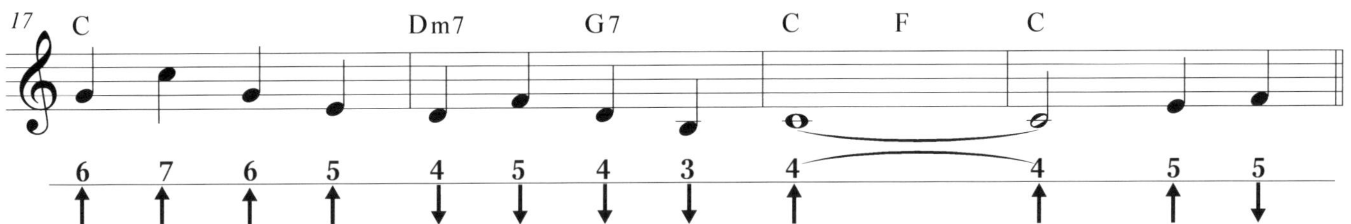
17
C
Dm7
G7
C
F
C
6 7 6 5 4 5 4 3 4 4 5 5

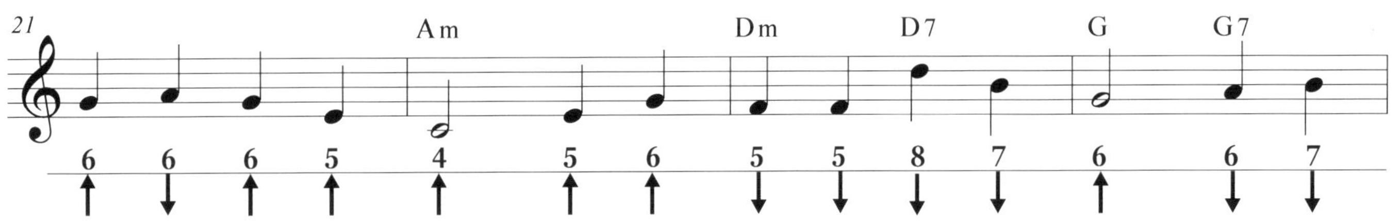
21
Am
Dm
D7
G
G7
6 6 6 5 4 5 6 5 5 8 7 6 6 7

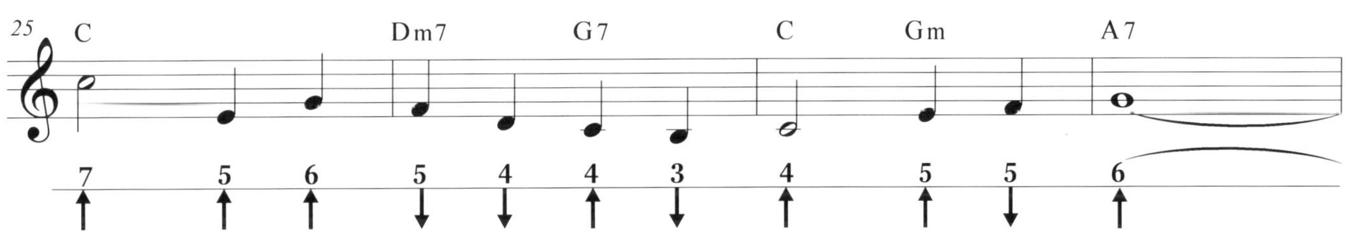
25
C
Dm7
G7
C
Gm
A7
7 5 6 5 4 4 3 4 5 5 6

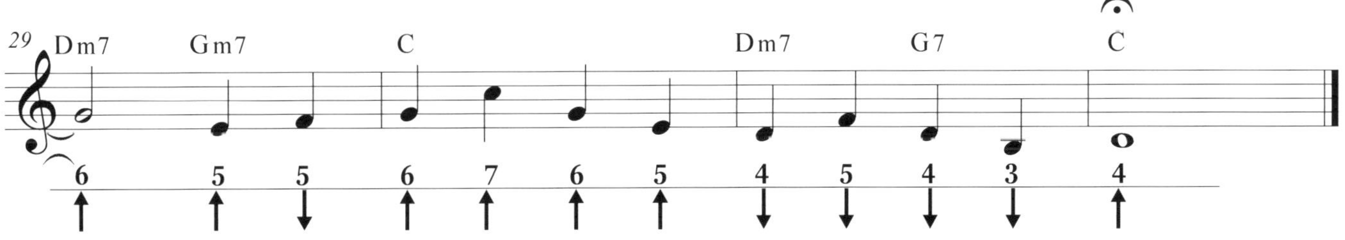
29
Dm7
Gm7
C
Dm7
G7
C
6 5 5 6 7 6 5 4 5 4 3 4

Auld Lang Syne

Even ♩ **= 110**

Old Scottish Melody

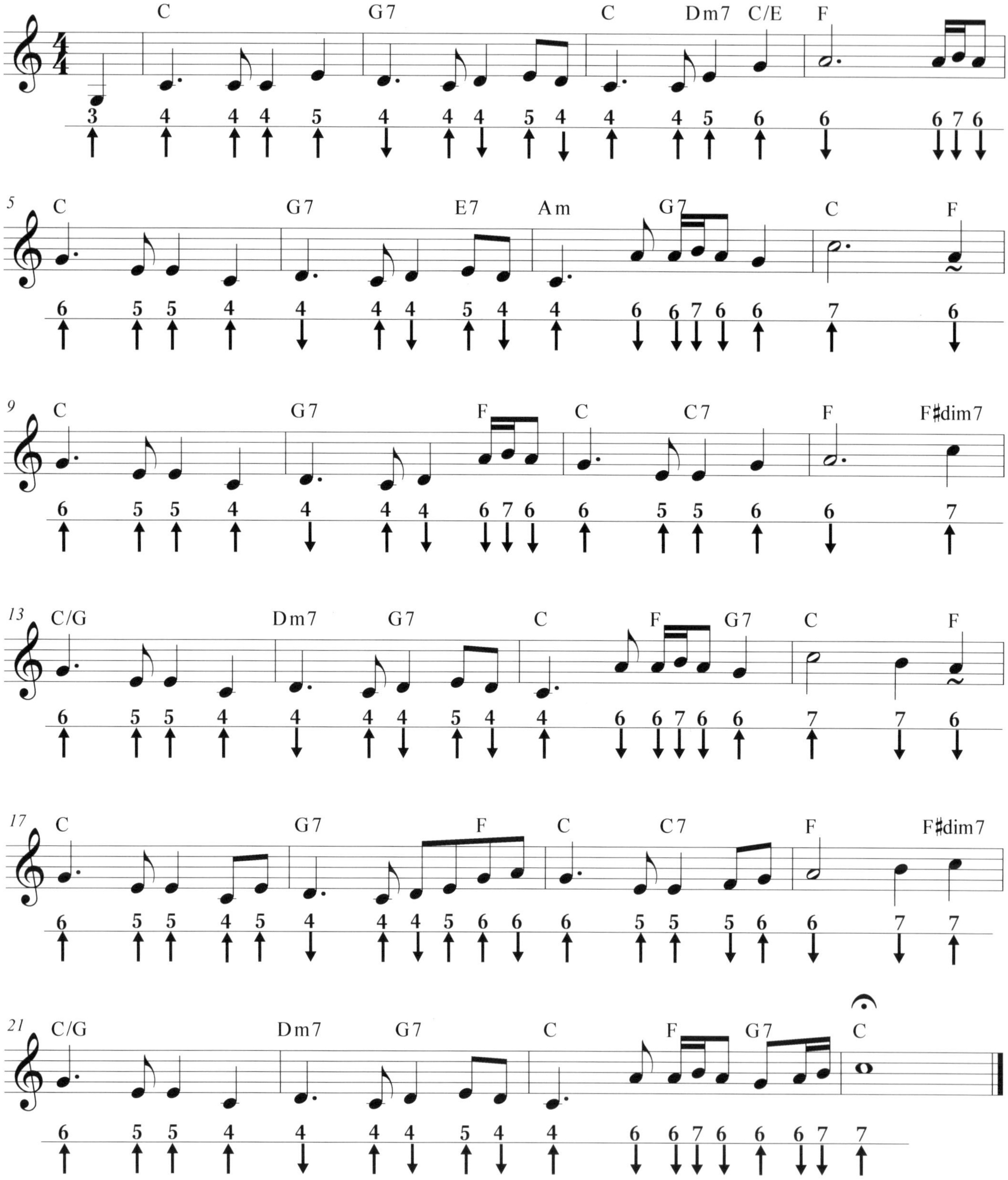